ALREADY PUBLISHED

PENGUIN
MODERN MASTERS

EDITED BY frank kermode

By Modern Masters we mean the men who
have changed and are changing the life and
thought of our age. The authors of these volumes are themselves masters, and they have
written their books in the belief that general
discussion of their subjects will henceforth be
more informed and more exciting than ever
before. —F.K.

antonin artaud

martin esslin

PENGUIN BOOKS

Penguin Books Ltd, Harmondsworth,
Middlesex, England
Penguin Books, 625 Madison Avenue,
New York, New York 10022, U.S.A.
Penguin Books Australia Ltd, Ringwood,
Victoria, Australia
Penguin Books Canada Limited, 2801 John Street,
Markham, Ontario, Canada L3R 1B4
Penguin Books (N.Z.) Ltd, 182–190 Wairau Road,
Auckland 10, New Zealand

First published in Great Britain
by Fontana Paperbacks 1976
First published in the United States of America by Penguin Books 1977

LIBRARY OF CONGRESS CATALOGING IN PUBLICATION DATA
Esslin, Martin.
Antonin Artaud.
(Penguin modern masters)
Bibliography: p.
Includes index.
1. Artaud, Antonin, 1896–1948.   2.   Authors, French
—20th century—Biography.
PQ2601.R677Z636   1977   841'.9'12   77–1269
ISBN 0 14 00.4368 3

Printed in the United States of America by
Offset Paperback Mfrs., Inc., Dallas, Pennsylvania
Set in Linotype Primer

Acknowledgment is made to the following
for material used:

GEORGE BORCHARDT, INC.: From *The Complete Works
of Antonin Artaud.*

HARCOURT BRACE JOVANOVICH, INC.: From
The Diary of Anaïs Nin, © 1966 by Anaïs Nin.
From *The Diary of Anaïs Nin*, Volume II.
Reprinted by permission of
Harcourt Brace Jovanovich, Inc.

Si je suis poète ou acteur ce n'est pas
pour écrire ou déclamer des poésies,
mais pour les vivre.

> ARTAUD, letter to Henri Parisot,
> 6 October 1945

— Vous délirez, monsieur Artaud.
  Vous êtes fou.

— Je ne délire pas.
  Je ne suis pas fou . . .

> ARTAUD, *Pour en finir avec le
> jugement de Dieu*

CONTENTS

PREFACE

Most books on Antonin Artaud hitherto available in English have concentrated on his theatrical theories and activity. The aim of this brief study is somewhat different: While dealing with his views on the theater at some length, it endeavors to set them within the wider framework of his importance as a cult figure, a revolutionary force, and a unique psychological case history.

Artaud's work and his life are inextricably interwoven; hence a good deal of the book is devoted to his biography. A full chronology of his life is given in the Biographical Note.

References to the collected edition of Artaud's work are given in the text; the title has been abbreviated as *OC* (i.e. *Oeuvres Complètes*), followed by the Roman numeral indicating the volume and Arabic figures giving the page. Quotations from the first two volumes are from the revised editions. All translations are mine.

I am grateful to Dr. R. D. Laing, with whom I have discussed some of the implications of Artaud's psychiatric history. Needless to say, all views on this subject expressed in the book are nevertheless my own.

M.E.

Master or Madman?

i

A few months before he died Antonin Artaud was
asked by the French radio service to prepare a
program for the series *La Voix des poètes*; he
wrote and recorded a radiophonic poem for four
voices, xylophone, and percussion which he called
Pour en finir avec le jugement de Dieu (*To Have
Done with God's Judgment*). It was due to be
broadcast on 2 February 1948, but on 1 February the Director General of the Radiodiffusion
Française banned it on the grounds that it was
blasphemous and obscene and would prove in-
tolerably offensive to the audience. Clearly the
intention also was that the recording of this
scandalous production should be destroyed. But
surreptitious copies were made and have sur-
vived. One of these—eventually recopied onto a
small cassette and therefore much deteriorated in
quality—is in my possession. And so I can listen
to Artaud's own voice as he recites his weird
and violent words and utters his wild, piercing,
inarticulate cries—outbursts of such a deep intensity of anguish beyond speech that they freeze

the blood: It is as though all human suffering, mankind's sum-total of dammed-up, frustrated rage, torment, and pain had been compressed into these tortured, primal shrieks.

It would be all too easy to dismiss these screams as no more than the demented ululations of a madman. That they contain an element of madness is beyond doubt; but there is far more in them than mere madness. Yet if they are not mere madness: what?

An answer to that question might furnish an explanation for the immense, surprising, and by no means easily comprehensible impact Artaud has had on the generation which has grown up since he died in 1948, an impact which certainly qualifies him to be regarded as one of the "modern masters," and which manifests itself in a number of different spheres: in the theater, certainly, but also in poetry, literary criticism, psychology, political ideology, philosophy, the drug cult, and the search for alternative life-styles. The very frequency with which Artaud's name is invoked in France, the United States, and many other Western countries makes him a figure whose influence must be recognized among the forces that shape the thinking and feeling of our time and, in some measure at least, contribute to its intellectual climate.

Yet if Artaud is among the modern masters, it is by no means easy to say into which of the recognized categories of achievement his contribution falls. He was not a *thinker* who could be regarded as having produced a coherent body of new knowledge; nor was he a *doer*, a man of action, a hero who shaped events and influenced the course of history; and while undoubtedly he was a *poet* of great power, it is not his poetry that accounts for his influence. His writings about the theater have had considerable influence, but his actual work in that sphere is generally acknowledged to have been a failure, so that he must be regarded as an inspiration for the work of others rather than a great director in his own right. In this he resembles those powerful figures who, while not producing anything like a tangible, verifiable system of thought, act as catalysts and stimulators for others by opening up new areas of speculation and directing attention toward new modes of seeing—prophets of new visions like Nietzsche or Marshall McLuhan. Like these, Artaud was the pioneer of a new approach, the inventor of a new vocabulary. This is a real and important contribution; but it still does not account for Artaud's wider, more profound influence in areas far removed from the theater.

Artaud, I feel, is, above all, an example of another, more mysterious type of personality with major influence and impact: one of those masters whose effect arises not so much from what they have achieved and *done* in concrete, tangible terms, but rather from what they *are* and what they have *suffered*. The influence of a powerful figure of this type ultimately derives from the image of himself he has left behind and which has, somehow, mysteriously, become the encapsulated embodiment, clear, compressed, immediately apprehended, of a whole complex of attitudes, ideas, and precepts contained within that image.

Such a personality radiates immense power and exercises far-reaching influence because his image has become a *symbol*, a concise poetic metaphor for his entire life, character, and teaching. When one thinks of Artaud one is immediately aware of his image, or rather of one or the other of the two images which have come to stand for him and his life experience: the beautiful, spiritual young monk who stands by Saint Joan as she mounts the stake in Carl Theodor Dreyer's film *La Passion de Jeanne d'Arc*, the lean, ascetic face with its deep burning eyes captured in overwhelming close-ups; or the furrowed, ravaged face of the wasted, toothless old man that stares out of the self-portraits which Artaud drew in the last years of his life after he had emerged from a decade of confinement as a lunatic. Both these images remain engraved on the memory. They are unforgettable.

Artaud is unique among great writers and prophets in that he was an actor in the cinema, so that his living, moving image remains as much with us as his recorded voice; and this has undoubtedly contributed to the emergence of his image as a power to be reckoned with and its crystallization into the symbol of an attitude to life. For let it not be said that such a man's appearance is of no account. Artaud, the theoretician of the theater who never tired of stressing the prime importance of the body's concrete reality as against the mere hot air of language and abstract thought, stands himself for the view that a man's looks may contain and express his essential truth. Would Che Guevara, an unsuccessful revolutionary and an unoriginal thinker, ever have acquired the influence he wielded among the young of the generation of 1968 had not his image, the beautiful, martyred face of his murdered body, captured the imagination and become the embodiment of a whole complex of doctrine, passion, and life-style?

Some such symbol-images may acquire their power by mere chance. Artaud's does not belong to these. He shaped his image deliberately, fully conscious of what he was doing. Between the face of the soulful young monk of 1928 and the toothless, ravaged martyr's visage of 1948 there lies a lifetime of suffering which Artaud regarded as his ultimate artistic achievement: "Tragedy on the stage is not enough for me, I am going to carry it over into my life," he told Jean-Louis Barrault in 1935.[1] He designed his life, took upon himself and endured his suffering as a deliberate creation, a work of art. And the double image which remains with us compresses and sums up his whole existence, *is*, in a certain sense, that work of art, or at least a metaphor for it.

Images of Man of such inner complexity, conciseness, and expressive force are the stuff that myths are made of. Some such images are created by history itself and distill it into all-embracing, universally understood

[1] Jean-Louis Barrault, *Souvenirs pour demain*, p. 104.

symbols: Saint Joan, the girl in soldier's garb riding at the head of liberating armies; Saint Sebastian pierced by arrows; Lenin orating, his head thrust forward, his arm raised in a fiery gesture. Other such myth-generating images are deliberate creations: Alfred Jarry turned into Ubu, an author who has become his own fiction; or Barbey d'Aurevilly, the eternal literary dandy, strolling through Paris with his lobster on a leash; or Chatterton, who made himself the image of the martyred young poet. Such images-turned-into-myth can grow into objects of worship. What they all, each on its own level, have in common is the mystery of *incarnation*: a body of ideas, precepts, experiences made concrete, become flesh; the story of a life and of a death compressed into one memorable picture capable of evoking an immediate emotional response. In such an image the word, the concept, is made palpable and becomes a physical presence. The incarnated Word, the Savior on the Cross, is the greatest and most powerful of all these symbols. But the phenomenon exists on a multitude of levels, down to the humblest and most trivial. At the opposite end of the spectrum, on the lowest rung of the ladder, stand the artificially created incarnations of the mass mind's aspirations, cult figures like James Dean or Marilyn Monroe.

Antonin Artaud, strangely, was both an actor *and* a prophet, an image on the flickering screen *and* a martyred saint, a figure in whom make-believe and profound aesthetic, philosophical, human insights mingle: a fine face, a sage, a teacher, and a lunatic, all in one.

With his exceptional lucidity—the lucidity of the madman, some say—Artaud himself never doubted that his impact as an artist and as a teacher depended on his being able to incarnate his teaching and his art in his personality: "Where others want to produce works of art, I aspire to no more than to display my own spirit. . . . I cannot conceive of a work of art as distinct from life," he proclaimed as early as 1925, before he had reached the age of thirty (*OC* 1, 61).

Any attempt to present or understand Artaud must, therefore, take his life as its starting point. He is the true existential hero: What he did, what happened to him, what he suffered, what he *was*, is infinitely more important than anything he said or wrote. Indeed so volatile, so contradictory are his opinions that it would be as easy to prove, by quotations from his published works or letters, that he was a deeply devout practicing Christian, as that he gloried in being a blaspheming atheist; that he preached violent revolution, as that he rejected all overt political action; that he saw salvation in sexual excess and the wildest indulgence of the senses, as that he regarded sexuality as the ultimate source of all the ills that beset mankind; that he was a leading surrealist, as that he considered the whole movement no better than a rabble of pretentious frauds; and, indeed, a whole row of further contradictory propositions. In fact, each such utterance can be understood only from the life situation, the existential context from which it sprang. It is futile to argue, as do those who regard Artaud as a useful prop of their particular cause, that he was lucid and in full command of his mental powers when he held the opinion they want to quote, and was utterly mad and unaware of what he was saying when he uttered the opposite view. The fact is that he held *all* his opinions with the same passionate sincerity at the moment he expressed them, and that it is impossible to draw a hard and fast line between his moments of "sanity" and those of his "madness," if, indeed, the concept of madness can be validly applied to a personality like Artaud at all.

But Artaud incarnates more, and more complex, concepts and problems than he himself could ever be aware of. His sufferings, for example, embody and exemplify, in an astonishingly clear and concentrated form, one of the most hotly debated and significant issues of our time: Artaud provides a focus and prime example for the controversy over the nature of insanity in which Michel Foucault in France and R. D. Laing and Thomas

Szasz in the English-speaking world play so prominent a part, a controversy which raises issues far wider than mental health and contains a fundamental critique of our whole society and mode of life. Similarly Artaud, the drug addict and victim of drugs, incarnated, long before these issues assumed their present importance, the whole complex and controversial problem of drugs and the drug culture.

There were times, during the years of his internment in various lunatic asylums, when Artaud was convinced that he was literally bearing the burden of the sins of all mankind; that he was starving because the people of the world were eating *his* food, that he was being poisoned by the sperm and excrement an entire impure world was unloading upon him. And when he finally succeeded in regaining his freedom, he identified himself with van Gogh, a great artist confined in lunatic asylums and driven to suicide by society. To our own time he has, even more so than van Gogh, become the embodiment of a lonely individual persecuted and victimized for his individuality and life-style by the upholders of convention and propriety. Hence his appeal to the radical, revolutionary Left. Persecuted, he replied with the rage of a ruthless persecutor. The immense, stored-up energies of boundless aggression which resound in the wild cries and screams on my tape are still fuelling the forces of radical dissent.

Such an ability to preserve and to release anew enormous psychic force is the hallmark of the true myth. Artaud, the incarnation of a multitude of ideas and experiences, is one of the archetypal, mythical heroes—or sacrificial victims—of our age. The creation of that myth and the image which embodies it is his life's achievement.

And—as with the heroes of all myths—the only way to gain access to an understanding of what he stands for, of what the image *means*, is to follow the story of the hero's life, martyrdom, and death.

The Road to Rodez

Antonin Marie Joseph Artaud was born at Marseilles—4, Rue Jardin des Plantes—at eight o'clock in the morning on 4 September 1896.

Antoine Roi Artaud, his father, was a prosperous *armateur* or shipping agent whose business consisted in chartering ships for the trade with the eastern Mediterranean, an area with which the family had close links. Artaud's paternal grandfather, Marius-Pierre Artaud, had married a Greek from Asia Minor, Cathérine Schili (whose name was also spelled Schily, Schiley, Chili, or Chilé). Artaud's mother, Euphrasie Nalpas, was the daughter of that Cathérine Schili's sister, Mariette Schili; his parents were thus first cousins, his two grandmothers sisters and he himself three-quarters Levantine Greek. Artaud remained deeply attached to his two grandmothers throughout his life. In his correspondence from the asylum at Rodez both make their appearance in the group of female figures—sometimes referred to as his daughters—whom he cherished with almost religious veneration.

In his childhood he occasionally accompanied his mother on her visits to Smyrna, where *her* mother, Mariette Nalpas, née Schili (whom the family called Miette, and Artaud himself Neneka), lived. It was during one of these visits that, at the age of ten, he is said to have almost drowned in the sea, an incident which left him with a lifelong fear and detestation of water. The Greek influence which pervaded Artaud's childhood can also be seen in the pet name by which he was known in the family, Nanaqui, derived from the Greek diminutive of his Christian name, Antonaki. He continued to use this name all his life and at times, when he strenuously denied that he was still Antonin Artaud, nevertheless remained Nanaqui to himself.

This link to the Levantine Greek world is more than a picturesque detail of Artaud's biography. It is a key factor in understanding his personality, outlook, and mode of thinking. For while undoubtedly Artaud was formed in part by the literary and theatrical life of Paris—his friendships and feuds with the surrealist circle and his contacts with the actors and directors around Dullin, Pitoeff, and Jouvet—the Levantine world we know through Cavafy or Durrell's *Alexandria Quartet* also contributed its share to his development. The flamboyance of his acting style and even the way he pronounced certain vowels have, at times, been attributed to his origins. Nor can it be without significance that the one woman who played a major part in his emotional life, the actress Genica Athanasiou (1897–1966), a Rumanian of Albanian-Greek origin, came from the same Levantine background. When Artaud published his first poems, in a little review he and some of his schoolfellows at the Collège du Sacré Coeur at Marseilles had started when he was about fourteen years old, he chose a pseudonym with a distinctly Greek flavor, Louis des Attides.

But the most striking expression of Artaud's immersion in the habits of thought and imagination of the Hellenistic world can be seen in the close affinity between his religious and cosmological fantasies in the last fifteen years of his life and the universe of the Hellenistic Gnostics, those numerous and diverse schools of philosophical and mystical speculation which flourished around the eastern Mediterranean between the third and seventh centuries. Condemned and strenuously opposed by the Christian Churches as pernicious heretics, these Gnostic philosophers, schools, and sects created a bewildering variety of syntheses between Christianity, Greek philosophy, and Eastern religious thought and myth. Just as Artaud did in his later writings, the Gnostics mingled elements from the canonical as well as apocryphal books of the Bible with Neo-Platonism and the Cabbala, Indian beliefs in the transmigration of souls, the Egyptian cult of Osiris and Horus, Manichaean teachings about the world as a duality of good and evil, Zoroastrianism from Persia, Babylonian astrology, which interprets the universe as a rigid hierarchy of ascending and descending spheres, and remnants of the classical Greek mystery religions like the cult of Dionysos and the mysteries of Orphism. In reading the writings of Artaud's final phase one is again and again struck by the parallels with Gnosticism. Like Marcion of Halicarnassus Artaud believed that the God who created our world must be wicked and incompetent—how else could he have made it so cruel and imperfect?—and that salvation could come only from a God outside our universe and therefore innocent of its creation. Like the Barbelo-Gnostics, who ritually spilled their sperm to break the endless cycle of sexual procreation, Artaud wanted to wean humanity away from the evil of physical sexuality; and like all the Gnostics he was obsessed with numerology, systems of divination, and the making and breaking of spells. Artaud's strange book on the Roman Emperor Heliogabalus is dedicated to Apollonius of Tyana, the Greek philosopher who travelled through Asia Minor, Babylonia, and India to merge Greek and Oriental doctrines. In his prophetic phase Artaud also saw himself as destined to reconcile Eastern philosophy and ritual with Western thought and art, and as an heir to the Hellenistic teachers and Magi who pursued the same ideal.

At the age of five Artaud fell severely ill. It is said that he had meningitis and that the disease left him with a nervous disability which remained with him all his life and was the source of most of his later sufferings. If this view is correct it would follow that Artaud's later psychological troubles had physiological causes. But such a connection should not too easily be taken for granted. Was the disease in question really meningitis? The diagnosis of meningitis was by no means certain in 1901; the term as used then covered a multitude of fevers and infections. Moreover, Artaud himself, although he spoke of having suffered from headaches and facial cramps from the age of six or eight, dated the onset of his nervous debility from puberty. In 1914, when he was eighteen, he fell into an acute depression during which he destroyed all his youthful writings. This seems to indicate a profound emotional crisis rather than a purely physiological nervous disorder.

There may be a link between this adolescent emotional upheaval and an episode which Artaud endowed with great significance when looking back on his youth from the asylum at Rodez: At the age of nineteen (in 1915 or 1916), he maintained, he had been knifed in the back by two pimps in a street in Marseilles, Cours Devilliers. Whether this actually happened or not— Artaud tended to construct an imaginary and highly dramatic past for himself at this period—it did have reality for him as a turning point in his life. In 1945 —thirty years later—he regarded it as the first manifestation of a vast conspiracy by powerful sects of "initiates" against him. The inner logic of this adventure, whether real or imaginary, seems to connect sexual guilt with the onset of the world's hostility toward him.

At Rodez Artaud claimed that the scar of that knife wound remained visible on his back. Whether he had been physically maimed or not, it was at about this time (1915/16) that he spent his first period in a sanatorium for nervous disorders at Rouguières near Marseilles.

The First World War was in its third year. After his return from the sanatorium Artaud, approaching the age of twenty, received his call-up papers. He spent nine months of 1916 in a military training camp at Digne, but eventually obtained his release from the army on medical grounds; he himself later used to say that it had been because of his sleep-walking.

Artaud's family tried desperately to obtain a cure for the nervous disability which prevented Artaud from embarking on a career. During the next three years he spent long periods in a succession of resorts and sanatoria: at Saint-Dizier near Lyons, Lafoux-les-Bains (Gard), Divonne-les-Bains (Ain), and Bagnères-de-Bigorre in the Pyrenees. At the end of 1918 he was put into the care of Dr. Dardel at a sanatorium at Le Chanet, near Neufchatel, in Switzerland. Here he remained for well over a year, and here too he is said to have started to take laudanum. That date, May 1919, marks another fateful milestone in Artaud's life: the beginning of his enslavement to drugs.

Artaud's stay in Switzerland differed from his earlier sojourns in watering places and sanatoria in that Dr. Dardel provided him with proper psychiatric care and treatment. As a result Artaud's state improved sufficiently to make it possible for him to go to Paris, where his ambition was to embark on a literary career. Dr. Dardel recommended that he should still remain under a degree of medical supervision and suggested that he might lodge with Dr. Edouard Toulouse, at that time head psychiatrist of the asylum of Villejuif. Dr. Toulouse was a pioneer of mental health and a man of high culture and a wide range of interests, literary and philosophical as well as scientific. As far back as 1912 he had created a literary periodical, *Demain*, aimed at promoting a fuller, more integrated life-style on the basis of a fusion of scientific and "moral" thought.

Dr. Toulouse, as his wife reported later, recognized in Artaud, whose father brought him to Paris in March 1920, "an exceptional being, of the race that produces a Baudelaire, a Nerval, a Nietzsche . . ." and, convinced that he was precariously balanced on a tightrope between genius and madness, decided to do his utmost to help him. Treating him as a member of the family, he gave him work which, while congenial, would not overtax him: revising the style of medical articles translated from the German, looking up facts in libraries; gradually he entrusted Artaud with the running of *Demain*. Here Artaud began to publish some of his poems, as well as contributing articles on a variety of subjects, such as a project for an improved form of the *Baccalauréat*, and theater and art notices.

This literary activity and Dr. Toulouse's connections in the artistic and intellectual circles of Paris opened doors for Artaud: He made the acquaintance of literary lions like the poet Max Jacob and met a number of prominent painters. And most important of all, Dr. Toulouse introduced him to Lugné Poe, the director of the Théâtre de l'Oeuvre. The dark young man with exquisite features greatly impressed Lugné Poe (the producer who had launched Jarry's *Ubu Roi* on the world in 1896, the year Artaud was born), and Artaud became attracted to the idea of becoming an actor. By the end of 1920 he felt well enough to break loose from the direct supervision of Dr. Toulouse and found himself lodgings in the 16th arrondissement. And Lugné Poe offered him a small part in a forthcoming production.

On 17 February 1921 Artaud made his first appearance as an actor; in Henry de Régnier's *Les Scrupules de Sganarelle* he had a nonspeaking role, a bourgeois waked from his slumbers by a disturbance in the night. Lugné Poe praised him for the originality of his make-up and the elegance of his movement which made him appear as "a painter who had strayed among actors."

Artaud did not remain long at the Théâtre de l'Oeuvre. He continued his editorial activity with *Demain*, wrote poems, and reviewed art exhibitions. In the summer he returned to Marseilles and spent a holiday with his family at Evian on Lake Geneva. Back in Paris in the autumn of 1921, he continued his efforts to become an actor.

Artaud's uncle, Louis Nalpas, his mother's brother, was an influential figure in the French cinema of the time, artistic director of the Société des Ciné-Romans, well known for producing novellettish films, the cinematic equivalents of the cheapest railway bookstall literature. Through Nalpas Artaud obtained an audition with the great actor Firmin Gémier (1869-1933), who had created the part of Ubu for Lugné Poe in 1896 and was a tireless champion of the idea of a theater for the people, which was realized after his death by Jean Vilar's creation of the Théâtre National Populaire. Gémier had appeared in films produced by Louis Nalpas's company and was thus willing to give his nephew an audition. He was impressed by the young man and recommended him to Charles Dullin, who was just about to form his workshop of actors, half theater school, half avant-garde ensemble, the Atelier. Dullin liked Artaud and offered him a place with the Atelier.

Charles Dullin, the outstanding French theater personality of the 1920s, a brilliant and highly intelligent director and an actor whose spirituality overcame the handicap of a far from impressive appearance, exercised a decisive influence on Artaud's thinking on the theater. He was one of the first theoreticians of a *total theater* in which gesture, mime, color, music, and movement would rival the dialogue in importance. Artaud had himself been thinking on similar lines. He waxed enthusiastic about a theater "in which there are no props. The Japanese are our immediate masters and inspiration, and in addition Edgar Poe" (*OC* III, 118). He was deeply impressed by Dullin's intention "that his performances should . . . give the impression of *things never seen before*. Everything takes place in the mind. The sets are even more stylized and deliberately shaped than at the Vieux Colombier. His idea is the Japanese actor who acts without props. . . . The Gods of the school are not Tolstoy, Ibsen, and Shakespeare but Hoffmann and Edgar Poe. Our first performance will display stern frenzy and demented sharpness. . . . It is, to say the least, curious that I with my tastes should have stumbled on an enterprise so closely linked with my own ideas" (*OC* III, 121).

In Dullin's troupe Artaud not only worked as an actor but also made use of his considerable talent as a draughtsman to design scenery and costumes.

Among the student-actors of the Atelier was Genica Athanasiou, a young Rumanian actress who had come to Paris in 1919, at the age of twenty-two, to make her way in the theater. Artaud fell wildly in love with her, and their tempestuous affair lasted for some seven years through a series of crises usually provoked by Artaud's by no means unjustified jealousy. His love for Genica was so intense, so filled with a metaphysical fervor toward totality, that she, a beautiful but mentally lazy and somewhat shallow woman, concerned about her career and wanting no more than a lover who could give her sexual fulfillment, could neither understand what he was after nor live up to it.

The year 1922 was one of intense professional activity for Artaud the actor and designer. Dullin's troupe went on tour as well as appearing in Paris at the Vieux Colombier and elsewhere. After having played Anselme in Molière's *The Miser* in February, Artaud appeared in two important parts on 2 March: In Alexandre Arnoux's

Moriano et Galvan, for which he had designed both the scenery and the costumes, he played the King of the Moors, Galvan; and, on the same evening, he also appeared as Sottinet in Regnard's *Le Divorce*. For the third spectacle of the same evening, Lope de Rueda's interlude *Les Olives*, he had designed the costumes. On 20 June he scored a critical success in another important part, Basilio, the King of Poland, in Calderón's *Life Is a Dream*; Dullin played Prince Sigismund and Genica Athanasiou Estrella. Artaud had also designed the costumes. One newspaper remarked of Artaud that he had managed to combine great simplicity with marvellous royal dignity.

For the summer Artaud returned to Marseilles where, at the Colonial Exhibition, he was deeply impressed by a troupe of Cambodian dancers who performed in a reconstruction of the Temple of Angkor, an experience which foreshadows the even more decisive experience of his discovery of Balinese Dance Theater at the Paris Colonial Exhibition of 1931.

In October Dullin finally moved into a permanent home for his theater, the building on the Place Dancourt on Montmartre which became famous as the Théâtre de l'Atelier. And again Artaud continued to play important roles. But he began to annoy Dullin by insisting on more and more bizarre interpretations of his parts. In Pirandello's *Pleasure of Honesty*, in which he was playing a member of the board of directors of a commercial enterprise, he appeared made up in the highly stylized manner of the classical Chinese theater. "A symbolical make-up slightly out of place in a modern comedy,"[1] was Dullin's view more than a quarter century later. In Alexandre Arnoux's *Huon de Bordeaux* Artaud played the Emperor Charlemagne. During a rehearsal he entered on all fours and crawled toward his throne like an animal. Dullin disagreed with this

[1] Letter from Dullin to Blin, *Cahiers de la Compagnie Renaud-Barrault*, No. 22-23, p. 20.

extravagant interpretation of the old emperor's character and tried to stop him. Artaud suddenly got up and said with a gesture of utter contempt: "Oh well! If you insist on truth!"

Nevertheless he achieved considerable success and earned Dullin's approval in some other productions, notably Cocteau's *Antigone*, which opened on 20 December 1922 and attracted *tout Paris*. Genica Athanasiou appeared in the title role, Artaud was Tiresias, and Dullin Creon. Picasso designed the set, Coco Chanel the costumes, the music was by Arthur Honegger. The first night, moreover, produced a typically Parisian scandal. Two different bands of opponents of Cocteau tried to stop the performance: Raymond Duncan, Isadora's brother, who felt that Cocteau had betrayed the true Greek spirit; and André Breton and his surrealists, who deplored Cocteau's descent into the world of fashion.

After his clash with Dullin over his interpretation of Charlemange Artaud left the Atelier and joined Georges Pitoeff's troupe at the Comédie des Champs-Elysées. Jean Hort, a Swiss actor also with Pitoeff at the time, describes him as looking barely older than twenty, although he was already approaching twenty-seven. But on stage, while acting, Hort says, his intensity, the feverish tension which stiffened his body, enabled him to appear much older, indeed any age he wanted. "I can still see," says Hort, "the pale color of his face, his shadowed cheeks in which repeated tensing had not yet cut permanent lines. His chestnut hair still grew deep into his forehead, which later, once it was bare, would look so remarkable. I can still see his blue-green eyes, often feverish, his frail body. . . . And his hands!"[2]

At the Comédie des Champs-Elysées Artaud appeared in a number of supporting parts: He was cast as the prompter in Pirandello's *Six Characters in Search of an Author* but failed to turn up at the final rehearsals and had to be replaced; later he was allowed to take up his

[2] Jean Hort, *Antonin Artaud, le suicide de la société*, p. 56.

part again; as Jackson in Leonid Andreyev's *He Who Gets Slapped*; and as a robot in Capek's *RUR*, directed by Kommissarjevsky. In 1923 and 1924 he also acted in two films: Claude Autant-Lara's *Faits divers* and Luitz-Morat's *Surcouf*, shot on location in Brittany in the summer of 1924; in this last he had the important part of a villainous traitor. An acting task which combined theater and film was the first performance of Ivan Goll's *Methusalem* at the Théâtre Michel, an avant-garde play which included filmed passages; in these, directed by Jean Painlevé, Artaud appeared as an officer, a bishop, and a country bumpkin.

While establishing himself as a man of the theater and making his mark in the cinema, Artaud continued his literary activity. His poems appeared in such periodicals as the *Mercure de France* and *Action* as well as in Dr. Toulouse's *Demain*. He edited an anthology of the writing of Dr. Toulouse, *Au fil des préjugés,* which was published in 1923. And D. H. Kahnweiler, the famous art dealer and publisher, whom he had met through his artist friends André Masson, Elie Lascaux, and Joan Mirò, issued Artaud's first book, a slim volume of poems, *Tric-Trac du ciel* (the title has been rendered as *Backgammon of the Heavens*, which sounds much less poetic than the French) in an edition limited to one hundred copies.

But the most important development, decisive for Artaud's entire career, was his famous correspondence with Jacques Rivière, the influential editor of the *Nouvelle Revue Française*, France's leading literary periodical. Artaud had sent some of his poems to the *NRF*, and on 1 May 1923 Rivière replied that he felt unable to publish them. Yet they had aroused his interest sufficiently so that he wanted to make their author's acquaintance: Could Artaud pass by at his convenience any Friday between four and six? On 5 June Artaud went to see Rivière. The same evening he wrote him a long letter in reply to the criticisms of his work which

Rivière had made during their conversation. Artaud admitted the weakness of his poems but went on to explain his peculiar difficulty:

> I am suffering from a terrible sickness of the spirit. My thought abandons me in all possible measure, from the simple fact of the thought itself to the external fact of its materialization in words. Words, the shape of sentences, the internal direction of thoughts, simple reactions of the mind—I am in constant pursuit of my intellectual being. When, therefore *I can take hold of a shape*, however imperfect, I set it down, out of fear that I might lose the whole idea. I am below my own level, I know it, I suffer from it, but I submit to it rather than die altogether. (*OC* 1, 30)

Artaud, it must be stressed, did not adduce this argument, that he suffered from a nervous disorder, in mitigation of a lack of talent. He drew Rivière's attention to the fact that what he wanted to say did not amount to a mere personal apologia but raised important general questions: Was writing which emerged from a tremendous struggle for expression and was therefore less than perfect in form and elegance really less deserving of publication than more facile but formally more perfect poems? Rivière's reply showed that he had not grasped this point at all. It merely reassured Artaud that with a little application he might well do better and get published in the *NRF*. More than six months later, on 29 January 1924, Artaud, who had obviously been pondering Rivière's insensitive consolatory remarks, returned to the attack: Were not the products of such a profound struggle for expression of real worth? "I am a man who has suffered much in his mind, and because of this *I have the right* to speak" (*OC* 1, 38). And he included a new poem, "Cri." No reply was received, and on 24 March 1924 Artaud curtly demanded the return of his letters and manuscripts. On the following day Rivière replied apologetically: he recognized the interest of Artaud's work, but, he asked, how was it possible, if Artaud really had such difficulties in catching the flow of his thought in the act of setting it down on paper, that in describing this very disability he could reach such heights of lucidity and eloquence? Rivière warned Artaud against literary theories which insisted on extreme spontaneity of expression, such as that of the surrealists, and advised him, in a rather patronizing manner, to work hard at trying to perfect his ability to translate his thoughts into formal patterns. The correspondence continued till 8 June and the upshot of it all was that Rivière suggested that, instead of publishing the poems Artaud had sent him, he should publish the correspondence about the *rejection* of the poems. Rivière wanted Artaud to remain anonymous, but Artaud insisted that nothing should be concealed.

The *Correspondence avec Jacques Rivière* appeared in the *NRF*'s issue for September 1924 and later as a book. It is of prime importance not merely because it made Artaud's name well known and enabled him to become a contributor to the most influential organ of the French intellectual elite, but above all because it marks the decisive breakthrough for his development as a writer. At last he had found a subject to write about: his own case, his disability, as a paradigm of the problem of art itself. Rivière's rejection had provoked him to examine his own problem and realize that his predicament was of general import and significance. Only a few months earlier, in a note in a small occasional periodical he had started in February 1923, *Le Bilboquet* (only two numbers ever appeared), Artaud had felt quite different about the problem of capturing thought in poetry and had, in effect, shared Rivière's view that it was all a matter of hard work and technique:

The supreme art consists in lending to the expression of our thought the rigor and truth of its original stratification through the cunning of a well-applied

rhetoric. . . . And the art consists in bringing this
rhetoric to the point of crystalization needed to achieve
a complete fusion with certain modes of being, real
ones, of the emotion and the thought. In a word:
The only enduring writer is the one who has been
able to make that rhetoric behave as though it *was*
the thought itself, and not just the outward form
(*geste*) of the thought. (*OC* 1, 269)

In the correspondence with Rivière, on the other hand,
Artaud not only acknowledged the fact that he found
it impossible to capture his emotion and his thought in
the act of writing (which would have been no more
than a personal, and highly regrettable, disability), but
insisted that writing which recorded that failure, or
indeed the impossibility of ever achieving complete
success in capturing the thought itself, transcended the
shallow and facile achievements of those who used
rhetoric to mask that impossibility. (There are close
parallels here to Samuel Beckett's attitude toward writing as a pursuit not of success but of a minimalization
of failure.)

The correspondence with Rivière revealed Artaud to
himself. For the first time he had found a theme of his
own to replace the conventional subjects of poetry:
organ grinders' monkeys, the freshly fallen snow, or
indeed Love. The new theme he had found was himself,
his own case. In the following year he published two
slim volumes of miscellaneous writings which clearly
show this shift toward his new subject matter. These
are *L'Ombilic des Limbes* (a title difficult to translate,
perhaps best rendered as *The Navel* [i.e. focal point or
center] *of Limbo*), which appeared in July 1925; and
Le Pèse-Nerfs (no easier to translate, perhaps, *Scales on
which to weigh one's nerves*), which followed in August.
The opening sentence of *L'Ombilic des Limbes* shows
how Artaud had moved away from the conventional
concept of the poet and man of letters: "Where others

want to produce works of art, I aspire to no more than
to display my own spirit" (*OC* 1, 61). And *Le Pèse-Nerfs*
contains repeated assertions of Artaud's newly won
awareness and pride of being a special case: "I am he
who has most closely experienced the numbing dislocation of his language in relation to his thought" (*OC* 1,
119); and his contempt for those whose main objective
is fine writing: "All writing is swinishness. People who
venture forth to try to put down in precise terms anything that goes on in their thought are swine." (*OC* 1,
120).

Artaud's formal adherence to the surrealist movement,
a few weeks after the publication of his correspondence
with Rivière, can also be seen as the direct and logical
consequence of this rejection of the conventional notion
of "literature." Once the laborious process of fixing
thought and emotion through the application of technique and skill, art, is unmasked as mere pretense and
sham; once the movement of the mind in forming
emotion and thought is recognized as more important
than elegance and refinement of expression, then automatic writing as preached, if not always practiced, by
the surrealists would be the answer. Artaud was introduced to the surrealists by André Masson. From October
1924 he began to take an active part in the surrealist
movement: He contributed to periodicals like *La Révolution Surréaliste* and *Disque Vert* and in January 1925
became director of the surrealists' Bureau de Recherches.
Apart from passionate discussions about the content of
the surrealist philosophy, the work of this research department consisted in collecting material (automatic
writing, dreams), trying to evolve "means and ways for
a surrealist investigation within the confines of surrealist thought" (*OC* 1, 344), and establishing criteria
by which authentically surrealist thought could be
recognized.

Artaud was nominated editor for the third issue of
La Révolution Surréaliste (15 April 1925) and himself

wrote a considerable number of the texts it contained. The cover announced boldly that 1925 was "The End of the Christian Era." Inside there were letters, written by Artaud to the Pope and the chancellors of Europe's universities, which rejected both Christianity and Western logic; they were followed by letters to the Dalai Lama and to the Buddhist schools, begging them to assist in the elimination of Western ways: "Teach us, O Lama, the material levitation of the body and how we can no longer be held down by the earth" (*OC* 1, 340); "Like you [the schools of Buddha] we reject progress: Come, and overthrow our habitations" (*OC* 1, 343).

While engaged in intense activity on behalf of the surrealists and in close personal contact with André Breton, Robert Desnos, Aragon, Eluard, Max Ernst, Raymond Queneau, and many other stimulating personalities, Artaud had to pursue his acting career in films. His father had died on 7 September 1924, a few weeks before he joined the surrealist group. This meant the cessation of financial help from Marseilles. Artaud's mother moved to Paris, where she lived in relatively modest circumstances. And Artaud had to earn his own living. The cinema seemed the likeliest source of a steady income, particularly as Artaud's uncle, who had helped him to gain a foothold in the industry, was pleased with his nephew's successes. In June 1925 Artaud spent some weeks in Italy on location for a film by Marcel Vandal (*Graziella*); in August he worked on Luitz-Morat's *Le Juif errant*. But the theater remained Artaud's main concern. Among the surrealists he encountered was the playwright Roger Vitrac, who shared many of Artaud's ideas and ambitions. In the course of 1926 they gradually formulated an idea for an avantgarde theater devoted to the exploration of dramatic ideas linked with the surrealist concept, a theater of the fantastic and grotesque, of dream and obsession, to be called Théâtre Alfred Jarry.

Vitrac, Artaud, and Robert Aron approached Dr. René

Allendy and his wife Yvonne on 26 September 1926 with a request for help in raising money for this venture. René Allendy is another of the enlightened psychiatrists (like Dr. Toulouse and later Dr. Ferdière at Rodez) who played such an important part in Artaud's life. A well-known psychoanalyst (Artaud briefly underwent some sessions of treatment with him in 1927), he was also interested in parapsychology and occultism and was head of a Groupe d'Etudes Philosophiques et Scientifiques pour l'Examen des Tendances Nouvelles at the Sorbonne. His wife, Yvonne, a woman of great charm and intelligence, was greatly interested in the arts. She decided to assist Artaud, Vitrac, and Aron (who acted as the administrator of the project) and succeeded in raising 3000 francs.

In its issue for November 1926 the *Nouvelle Revue Française* (edited, after the death of Jacques Rivière in February 1923, by Jean Paulhan, who became a close friend of Artaud's and played an important part in his life) published the First Manifesto of the Théâtre Alfred Jarry. This already contains a good many of Artaud's later ideas about a theater of cruelty. If theater is merely play, the world is too serious a place to indulge in it. "If the theater is not just play, if it is a true reality, by what means can we give it that degree of reality, make each performance a kind of event? That is the problem we have to solve" (*OC* II, 19). As an example of the kind of spectacle which is both theatrical and real, the manifesto cites a police raid on a brothel, with the balletlike deployment of the force surrounding the premises, followed by the procession of the arrested whores being led away like cattle to the slaughter. "This is what we want to arrive at: that at each performance we take a grave risk, that the whole interest of our effort lies in its seriousness. It is not to the mind or the senses of our audience that we address ourselves, but to their whole existence. Theirs and ours" (*OC* II, 21). So that ultimately the audience "will go to the theater as [they] go to the surgeon or the dentist" (*OC* II, 15). The leaflet issued by the new group to announce its first season (1926/27) promised, among other things, several hitherto unperformed plays by Jarry, *The Revenger's Tragedy* by Tourneur, and Strindberg's *Dream Play*. Not all of these projects came to fruition.

The preparations for the Théâtre Alfred Jarry brought Artaud into conflict with the surrealists. As early as September 1925, less than a year after he had joined them, Artaud wrote to Genica Athanasiou that he had received a hectoring letter from Breton "about Vitrac, in which he treats him as a villain and more or less orders me to break with him."[3] Vitrac had quarrelled with Eluard and had been expelled by the surrealists in December 1924. As Artaud's association with Vitrac became closer, the surrealists began to taunt him for his supposed commercialism in continuing to appear as a film actor and in trying to launch a theatrical enterprise of his own. And when Breton and his followers decided to convert the purely literary surrealist revolution into a political one and announced their collective adherence to the Communist party, the break became unavoidable.

At the end of November 1926, at a meeting held in the café Le Prophète, Artaud and Philippe Soupault were formally expelled by the surrealists. The language used about Artaud in the official document listing his transgressions is extremely strong. Calling him a man animated by a veritable beastliness, they charged "that he wanted to see in the Revolution no more than a change of the internal conditions of the soul, an attitude which belongs to the feeble-minded, the impotent, and the cowardly. Never, in whatever field, did his activity [he was also a film actor] constitute anything but concessions to nullity. . . . Let us leave him to his disgusting mixture of dreams, vague assertions, pointless insolence,

[3] Antonin Artaud, *Lettres à Genica Athanasiou*, p. 208.

and manias" (*OC* I, 445). As a final insult the document hinted that Artaud was not beyond committing
the ultimate transgression, reconversion to the Christian
faith. Although this actually happened some ten years
later, the only grounds for assuming such a step in 1926
were some contacts Artaud had had with Jacques
Maritain.

This document was not made public at the time. But
Breton, Aragon, Eluard, Péret, and Unik jointly signed
a pamphlet, probably written by Breton, *Au grand jour*
(*In Broad Daylight*), in which they announced their
adherence to the Communist party and the expulsion
of Artaud and Soupault. Artaud replied, in the summer
of 1927, in a pamphlet of his own, *A la grande nuit ou
Le Bluff surréaliste*, in which he hit back with equal
ferocity: "Did not surrealism die the day when Breton
and his adepts thought they had to join communism and
to seek, in the realm of fact and matter, the fulfillment
of an endeavor which could not normally develop any-
where but in the inner recesses of the brain?" (*OC* I,
364). Artaud insisted that the social, material, *external*
plane was of no interest to him because it was only a
pale reflection of inner realities.

In spite of the bitterness of these exchanges, Artaud's
name still occasionally made an appearance in surrealist
publications. And to the end of his life André Breton
was one of the people he remained most attached to, and
who played an important part in his fantasy life at
Rodez.

Film acting, so despised by the surrealists, continued
to occupy and maintain Artaud in funds. The year 1927
brought him two of his most famous roles: Marat in
Abel Gance's *Napoléon* and the part of the friar who
accompanies St. Joan to the stake in Carl Theodor
Dreyer's great film *La Passion de Jeanne d'Arc*. He also
appeared as a young intellectual soldier in Léon Poirier's
Verdun, visions d'histoire and was much attacked for
this by the Left intelligentsia of Paris, as the film had

been launched with official support as a patriotic work. He also became interested in the cinema as an art form which might be used to realize some of the ideas of the surrealists. In November 1927 the *Nouvelle Revue Française* published his script for such a film, *La Coquille et le clergyman* (*The Seashell and the Clergyman*), which actually went into production under the direction of Germaine Dulac, one of the earliest women directors in the history of the cinema. But Artaud was deeply dissatisfied with Dulac's approach to his script, which, although bizarrely unrealistic, he wanted to have treated as real, but which she had transformed into a series of dream images. When the film was shown for the first time at the Studio des Ursulines on 18 February 1928, Artaud and some of his friends tried to stop the performance by shouting insults about the director. Later, when Buñuel's *L'Age d'Or* and *Le Chien Andalou* and Cocteau's *Le Sang d'un poète* were hailed as pioneer works of a cinema of dream images, Artaud angrily drew attention to the fact that his film had preceded all these and was, in fact, much better than any of them.

In the meantime the Théâtre Alfred Jarry had come into being. It had neither a permanent company nor a permanent home and consisted of no more than its three initiators, who planned, from case to case, to present their productions with ad hoc companies in theaters hired for a few evenings. The first presentation was a triple bill: a short play, *Gigogne*, by Max Robur (pseudonym for Robert Aron); a musical joke by Artaud, *Le Ventre brûlé ou la Mère folle*, the text of which has been lost (it is said to have been a humorous treatment of the conflict between the cinema and the theater, one critic describing it as "a short hallucination with hardly any text in which the author has condensed a synthesis of life and death" and adding that "it left an extremely strong and persistent impression of strangeness" [*OC* IV, 380]); and a major surrealist, or rather proto-absurdist, play by Vitrac, *Les Mystères de l'amour*. Rehearsals started in May 1927 in the Théâtre de l'Atelier, which Dullin had put at the group's disposal; the performances were to be at the Théâtre de Grenelle, in which only one final rehearsal could be held during the night before the opening.

The two performances of this first production of the Théâtre Alfred Jarry took place on 1 and 2 June 1927. The press was by no means unfavorable, but it would be an exaggeration to say that the venture had an impact much greater than similar experimental showcase productions usually had in Paris. Aron was left with a deficit of almost 7000 francs, which he covered out of his own pocket.

But while Artaud tried to earn his living in films, the activities of the Théâtre Alfred Jarry continued. On 14 January 1928 it mounted its second presentation at the Comédie des Champs-Elysées. This was an even more curious mixture. One half of the program consisted of the uncut version of Pudovkin's film version of Gorki's *The Mother*, a masterpiece of the Soviet cinema which had been banned by the censor. The other half of the evening was a stage presentation of what was announced as "one act of a play, the name of whose author we are withholding, and who, incidentally, has not authorized us to perform it." Taken out of context the long dialogues of this fragment of a play appeared incomprehensible and boring to the audience, who became restless and loudly voiced their dissatisfaction. The play was in fact the third act of Claudel's *Partage de midi*, and the intention, clearly, was to expose its wordiness and boredom and to hold it up to ridicule. André Breton, who was in the audience, was among the first to realize this, and shouted: "Shut up, you idiots, this is by Claudel!" After the curtain had come down, Artaud appeared in front of it and announced: "The play is by Paul Claudel, Ambassador of France—who is an infamous traitor!" The surrealists, who were present in force, were in raptures, and it looked as though they would forgive Artaud many past sins and insults. But the rest of the audience and the establishment press were deeply scandalized and indignant. So also was the *Nouvelle Revue Française*, Claudel's publisher, whose copyright had been breached and to whom Artaud owed so much for publicizing his theatrical venture. Even Artaud's relationship with Genica Athanasiou suffered. He had made her act the part of Ysé without letting her know who had written the play, and had quarrelled with her over the interpretation of the text. On the other hand, the scandal had achieved one objective: It had made Artaud and his enterprise well known.

If scandal was the objective, the next venture of the group again attained it. But this time it was not the establishment but the surrealists who were scandalized. Artaud had from the very beginning planned to produce Strindberg's *Dream Play*. Mme. Allendy had friends among the Swedish colony in Paris, and it was suggested that the Swedish Embassy might subsidize the production of a play by a great Swedish writer. Artaud agreed. He secured an excellent cast which included Tania Balachova, Raymond Rouleau, and Etienne Decroux (later to become famous as a great mime). Two performances were planned, to be held on 2 and 9 June 1928 at the Théâtre de l'Avenue. The first of these was a brilliant society occasion: The Swedish ambassador, Prince George of Greece, the Duchess of Rochefoucauld, Paul Valéry, and hosts of foreign journalists were present. But so were some thirty surrealists, who occupied the front rows of the stalls. Furious that Artaud had accepted subsidies from a foreign government and allied himself with the cream of society, these surrealist interlopers hurled insults at the actors about being in the pay of Swedish capitalism. Artaud replied from the stage that he had agreed to produce the play only because Strindberg himself had been a victim of the Swedish establishment. At this some Swedes walked out of the theater. It was a memorable scene.

But worse was to come—from the surrealists' point of view the ultimate in abject treason on Artaud's part. The second performance was to be held a week after the first one, as a matinée on 9 June. Artaud and Aron, afraid that the disturbances would recur, announced that they were resolved to employ all means at their disposal to stop such a repetition. And these means consisted of—the police. Breton, Sadoul, Unik, and other surrealists were arrested at the entrance. And, according to Breton, Artaud himself was at the door, pointing out his erstwhile friends to *les flics*.

Robert Aron had had enough. He withdrew. But Vitrac and Artaud soldiered on to mount one more production. This was Vitrac's own play *Victor ou Les Enfants au pouvoir*, without doubt the only truly important new play presented by the Théâtre Alfred Jarry. This brilliant piece, which presents the plot of a conventional French bedroom farce as seen through the eyes of a hyperintelligent child unable to fathom the mysteries of sex which prompt his elders to behave in such an irrational fashion, gave Artaud an excellent opportunity to shine as a director. Tania Balachova was again to be in the cast. But the actress, who was to play Ida Mortemart, the beauty afflicted with an irrepressible urge to fart, withdrew in horror. In a letter (also printed in the program) Artaud explained to her replacement, Domenica Blazy, that this character represents the intrusion of the sordid side of matter into the realm of spiritual beauty. *Victor* was given three performances at the Comédie des Champs-Elysées, on 24 and 29 December 1928 and 5 January 1929. Many of the critics were shocked; very few saw the power and originality of the play and production. One of them gave it curious conditional praise: *If* it were true that *Ubu Roi* was a masterpiece, then *Victor*, which could be regarded as a kind of sequel to *Ubu*, might also be seen as a masterpiece! Foreign correspondents in Paris, less committed to the conventions of the French theater, saw the matter more clearly. Paul Block of the *Berliner Tageblatt* called it the most curious theatrical experience he had had in eight years as a correspondent in France; and the correspondent of *Lidove Noviny* of Prague clearly saw that the *leitmotiv* of Victor was the human condition itself, subject as it is to being soiled by the impurity of matter.

Victor, the fourth production of the Théâtre Alfred Jarry, was also its last. The Vicomte de Noailles gave Artaud another 20,000 francs in November 1929 to enable him to carry on, but even this sum proved insufficient. For the next six years Artaud desperately tried to regain an opportunity to direct a play on the Paris stage. And when he finally succeeded, in 1935, it led to catastrophe for him.

Having suffered a defeat in the theater, Artaud fell back on the cinema. He desperately needed money, not least to enable him to relaunch his theatrical ventures. He had hopes of selling some film scripts and, through these, breaking into film production. With this aim in mind he wrote a film treatment of R. L. Stevenson's *The Master of Ballantrae* (which he registered with the Association des Auteurs de Film on 26 April 1929) and made a free translation of M. Lewis's Gothic novel *The Monk*, published as a book in 1931. None of these film projects ever materialized. But Artaud's acting career continued. He appeared in an adaptation of Zola's *L'Argent*, directed by Marcel Herbier, and spent several months in the spring of 1929 in Nice, playing the part of a gypsy in Raymond Bernard's highly successful epic *Tarakanova*. In the early years of talking pictures some European companies produced their films in two versions in different languages, using the same sets and costumes. This practice was particularly popular in Germany, and Artaud went to Berlin several times to take part in the French versions of German productions. One of these, in 1930, was G. W. Pabst's film of Brecht's *Threepenny Opera*. The version of this classic which is usually shown is the German one with Rudolf Forster as MacHeath and Carola Neher as Polly. But a French version of the *Opéra de Quat' Sous* also exists with Albert Préjean as Mack the Knife. In this version Artaud plays the young man at the very beginning of the film who asks Peachum to join his organization of beggars and is shown the methods by which human pity can be aroused. Artaud's life thus touches that of Brecht. Like Brecht, Artaud disliked Pabst's adaptation of the play; but he admired Brecht's work.

Artaud found Berlin fascinating. "If I did not suffer from my perpetual headaches," he wrote to Dr. Allendy in July 1930, "I should greatly enjoy the life of Berlin, a city of astonishing luxury and frightening licentiousness. I am constantly amazed by what I see. They carry their obsession with eroticism everywhere, even into the shop-windows, in which all the dummies thrust their bellies forward" (*OC* III, 193). Artaud made several more visits to Berlin between 1931 and 1935. During the war, at Rodez, he claimed that he had met Hitler in the Romanisches Café, the meeting place of actors and intellectuals. This may well have been no more than one of the fantasies in which he indulged at that period in the asylum. But it may well also have been true. There is no reason why Hitler should not have occasionally been seen in the Romanisches Café.

The films in which Artaud was cast became worse and worse (he worked mainly for Raymond Bernard, Tristan Bernard's son—*Faubourg Montmartre, Les Croix de bois*—and Marcel Herbier—*La Femme de nuit*); and he did not get enough work in the cinema to give him an acceptable income. So his struggle to make a living became more and more desperate. As far back as March 1928 he had been invited by Dr. Allendy's study group to lecture at the Sorbonne on *Art and Death*; a year later Robert Denoël published a little book with the same title, *L'Art et la mort*, which contains a number of texts which had previously appeared in periodicals. Only the opening meditation had not previously been published, but it seems too short to have formed a complete lecture and may merely be a fragment of that lecture. It is chiefly remarkable for extolling the utility of drugs to recreate that state of mind of extreme lucidity of which children alone are spontaneously capable.

Artaud also contributed short notes and reviews to the *Nouvelle Revue Française* and even wrote, to make some money, fake first-hand reports of the Galapagos Islands and the brothels of Shanghai for the magazine *Voilà*.

Yet he never lost sight of his main objective: to revolutionize the theater. In July 1931 he visited the Colonial Exhibition in the Bois de Vincennes and had one of the key experiences of his life: On the terrace of the Indonesian temple which housed the exhibit of the Dutch colonial empire he saw a performance of Balinese dancing. Artaud was deeply moved: Here all his ideas of a nonverbal, magical theater of light, color, and movement seemed realized. His article on the Balinese theater, which appeared in the *Nouvelle Revue Française* for October 1931, initiated a series of theoretical essays on the theater, some originally delivered as lectures at the Sorbonne, which later formed the basis of Artaud's most influential book, *The Theater and Its Double*.

From 1931 Artaud embarked on a desperate search for the means to start his own theater. At the beginning of 1932 he succeeded in persuading Louis Jouvet to allow him to assist in the production of a play by Alfred Savoir, *La Patissière du village*. But Artaud spoiled his chances of gaining a foothold in an established theater by putting forward extravagant ideas which that conventional play simply could not support. In a letter to Jouvet (5 February 1932) he suggested that in the dream scene at the end of the play some twenty giant puppets, each more than fifteen feet in height, should appear, swaying to the tune of a military march made strange by the admixture of oriental harmonies, while Bengal fireworks exploded all around them. These puppets should each carry a symbolical object: One of them, for example, could have the Arc de Triomphe on its shoulders. No wonder that Jouvet got frightened and dropped Artaud.

Undaunted, Artaud approached Dullin and suggested that he should be allowed to direct Buechner's *Woyzeck*, one of his favorite plays. In a letter dated 7 March 1932 to Jean Paulhan, the editor of the *NRF* who had collaborated on the translation of *Woyzeck*, Artaud mentions this plan and adds that he had found a patron who might give money toward a project "which might be for the theater what the *NRF* is for literature." Artaud felt that this patron, M. de Grinief, director of the Comptoir National Cinématographique, could be persuaded to finance the venture if it found the support of the leading intellectuals around the *NRF*, André Gide, Paul Valéry, Valéry Larbaud, Julien Benda, and, of course, Paulhan himself, as well as Gaston Gallimard, the head of the *NRF* publishing enterprise. Paulhan was not unsympathetic. He agreed to publish an article by Artaud which would be a program and manifesto for such a new theater.

But the whole project was prematurely leaked to the press. On 26 June 1932 the *Intransigeant* published an article by Henri Philippon headed *Le Théâtre de la NRF* in which he reported rumors that the *NRF* had decided to open a theater and that they had, after much heart-searching, chosen Artaud to direct it:

It was at the Café des Deux-Magots that I had the good fortune of running into M. Antonin Artaud.

I hear whispers that the *Nouvelle Revue Française* wants to start a theater. Is that true?

Evidently, I myself am to run it. In a forthcoming number of the *NRF* I shall be publishing a kind of manifesto which André Gide, Julien Benda, Albert Thibaudet, Jean Paulhan, and Jules Supervielle will countersign. They will form the committee of honor. (*OC* v, 298)

On the following day the *Intransigeant* published a letter from Artaud headed "The Theater I am about to start" in which he explained some of his ideas more fully and also tactfully suggested that it was not the *NRF* who had initiated the project, and that *he* was doing so with the assistance of some of the writers connected with the journal. But the harm had been done. Gallimard was furious and Artaud had to apologize to him. Nevertheless the *NRF* did publish the first "Manifesto of the Theater of Cruelty" in its October issue.

There had been much debate between Paulhan and Artaud about the name by which Artaud's venture should be known. Artaud had written an article for publication in the journal *SUR* of Buenos Aires with the title *Le Théâtre alchimique* (The Alchemical Theater). Paulhan thought that might be a better name; he also suggested Theater of the Absolute or Metaphysical Theater. But Artaud insisted on Theater of Cruelty.

The response to this manifesto was, to say the least, lukewarm. Bernard Steele, the publisher, tried to launch a Societé Anonyme du Théâtre de la Cruauté with a total capital of 100,000 francs in 100-franc shares. Later, after the publication of Artaud's "Second Manifesto of the Theater of Cruelty," the projected share capital was raised to 650,000 francs. But this was even less successful.

To provide material for his theatrical enterprise, should it ever come to fruition, Artaud worked on a number of outlines of productions that would fit in with his ideas. In 1932 he was busy on an adaptation of Seneca's tragedy *Atreus and Thyestes*; in 1933 he produced a scenario for *La Conquête du Mexique*, which he read, to raise funds, at a soirée Lise Deharme gave for him in her home on the Quai Voltaire on 6 January 1934. He was also thinking of a play based on Shelley's *Les Cenci*.

Artaud's liaison with Genica Athanasiou had come to an end after the quarrel over *Partage de midi* at the beginning of 1928, but he continued to see her sporadically. In 1930–31 he lived for a time with Josette Lusson, an actress who had also been connected with the Théâtre Alfred Jarry. But this liaison too ended when he discovered that she—"my so-called wife"—had deceived him. In 1933 he met Anaïs Nin, who was studying psychoanalysis with Dr. Allendy, and fell in love with her. In her diary for March 1933 Anaïs Nin gives a vivid picture of Artaud at this period of his life:

Artaud. Lean, taut. A gaunt face with visionary eyes. A sardonic manner. Now weary, now fiery and malicious. The theater, for him, is a place to shout pain, anger, hatred, to enact the violence in us. . . . He is the drugged, contracted being who walks always alone, who is seeking to produce plays which are like scenes of torture. His eyes are blue with languor, black with pain. He is all nerves. Yet he was beautiful acting the monk in love with Joan of Arc in the Carl Dreyer film. The deep-set eyes of the mystic, as if shining from caverns. Deep-set, shadowy, mysterious . . . Allendy had told me that he had tried to free Artaud of the drug habit which was destroying him. All I could see that evening was his revolt against interpretations. He was impatient with their presence, as if they prevented him from exaltation. He talked with fire about the Kabala, magic, myths, legends.[4]

Artaud, who at that time was writing his book on Heliogabalus, wrote Anaïs Nin long love letters. She noted in her diary (May 1933): "Such an immense pity I have for Artaud, because he is always suffering. . . . Physically I could not touch him, but the flame and genius in him I love."[5]

In June Anaïs Nin met Artaud in a café. He asked her: "People think I am mad. Do you think I am mad? Is that what frightens you?" She goes on: "I knew at

4 *The Diary of Anaïs Nin,* Vol. I, pp. 195-96.
5 Ibid., p. 232.

that moment, by his eyes, that he was, and that I loved his madness. I looked at his mouth, with the edges darkened by laudanum, a mouth I did not want to kiss. To be kissed by Artaud was to be drawn towards death, towards insanity."[6] "Artaud," Anaïs Nin continues,

> sat in the Coupole, pouring out poetry, talking of magic. "I am Heliogabalus, the mad Roman emperor," because he becomes everything he writes about. In the taxi he pushed back his hair from his ravaged face. The beauty of the summer day did not touch him. He stood up in the taxi and, stretching out his arms, he pointed to the crowded streets: "The revolution will come soon. All this will be destroyed. The world must be destroyed. It is corrupt and full of ugliness. It is full of mummies, I tell you. Roman decadence. Death. I wanted a theater that would be like a shock treatment, galvanize, shock people into feeling." For the first time it seemed to me that Artaud was living in such a fantasy world that it was for himself he wanted a violent shock, to feel the reality of it, or the incarnating power of a great passion. But as he stood and shouted and spat with fury, the crowd stared at him and the taxi driver became nervous.[7]

Heliogabalus (*Héliogabale ou L'Anarchiste couronné*) is a strange book. If Artaud's identification with the Roman emperor is to be believed—and there are a number of critics who regard the book as autobiographical in a deep sense—his concept of his own life as an incarnation of ideas that could not be expressed in words alone would be powerfully confirmed. He saw Heliogabalus, a homosexual who wanted to be a woman and yet was the priest of the masculine principle, the incarnation of the Sun as well as the Moon, as "the paradigmatic image of this kind of dissociation of principles; the most clearly visible image of religious mania, of perversity

6 Ibid., pp. 238-39.
7 Ibid., p. 71.

and lucid folly, the image of all human contradictions."
(*OC* VIII, 74-75).

During 1934 Artaud had some further roles in films:
In the summer of that year he went to southern Algeria
to play the part of the emir Abd-el-Kader in a musical
based on an operetta about the conquest of Algeria in
the 1840s, *Sidonie Panache*, produced by his cousin
Alex Nalpas. The comedian Bach played the lead, while
Artaud rolled his eyes and fumed as the villain of the
piece. Another historical figure he portrayed was Savonarola in Abel Gance's *Lucrèce Borgia*. Fritz Lang
gave him a part in an adaptation of Molnár's *Liliom*
and Maurice Tourneur put him into another historical
epic, *Koenigsmarck*.

By February 1935 the manuscript of *Les Cenci* was
ready. Artaud gave a reading of it at the home of Jean-
Marie Conty. The play, a four-act tragedy in prose, was
full of blood and thunder, rape, incest, and murder.
Francesco Cenci is a historical figure, a Roman Renaissance aristocrat who had figured in a number of famous
and scandalous cases before the papal courts. He raped
his own daughter, Beatrice, and was murdered, allegedly
on the instigation of the victim of the rape, Beatrice,
together with his wife, Lucrezia. Stendhal had published an account of the affair, closely based on the
actual trial records. And Shelley had written a five-act
verse tragedy about it. Artaud's play is based mainly on
Shelley's text, somewhat shortened and reworked. The
mad count, who rapes his daughter not so much for lust
but because he wants to condemn her to eternal dam-
nation through incest, clearly was a tremendous part;
and so was that of Beatrice, the innocent victim roused
to take bloody vengeance and then condemned to death.

Fortunately—or unfortunately—for Artaud, there was
an actress interested in just such a part: an aristocratic
lady with strong financial backing in Paris society
named Iya Abdy, a delicate blonde beauty of Russian
origin who had become Lady Abdy when she married

Sir Robert Abdy, the fifth baronet of that name, whom, however, she had divorced after five years of marriage in 1928. Lady Abdy had little experience on the stage, but she wanted to become an actress. She and Robert Denoël, the publisher of some of Artaud's writings, found the financial backing for a production of *Les Cenci* as the first venture of Artaud's Theater of Cruelty.

At last Artaud had an opportunity to realize at least some of his ambitions, although he insisted that this first production could by no means be regarded as a full embodiment of his theories. But it was a first step.

Much of Artaud's preparatory work in mounting *Les Cenci* was inspired and original. But he also made some grave mistakes. Foremost among these was the choice of the venue for the experiment: The only theater readily available was the Théâtre des Folies-Wagram (later renamed Théâtre de l'Etoile), built, as the name implies, as a music hall, a large cavernous place, surrounded by a *promenoir* and approached through a narrow corridor-like foyer. Although this was clearly most unsuitable and constituted a grave handicap for the production, Artaud decided to take it. He would use the foyer for an exhibition about the Balinese theater and everything would work out fine.

André Frank, who acted as administrator for the enterprise, has described the period of rehearsals. Many of the actors did not grasp Artaud's new and original ideas. And "if his views on the theater were astonishing in their rigor and richness, his actual work in the theater, however, was far removed from the expected. Perhaps the gap that had to be bridged between the theater as it then was and the so-called Theater of Cruelty was too large; he was many years ahead of the time for it."[8] Artaud sensed all this. He became nervous and his nervousness transmitted itself to the actors.

[8] André Frank in *Lettres d'Antonin Artaud à Jean-Louis Barrault*, p. 65.

Some of them greatly profited by working for Artaud, chief among them Roger Blin, who acted as production assistant and played one of the two deaf-and-dumb murderers; he became one of Artaud's most loyal friends during the years of his confinement and was destined to emerge as a major figure of the postwar avant-garde theater, a pioneer for the work of Adamov and Beckett. Jean-Louis Barrault, who was assisting him with the production, had been cast by Artaud as Beatrice's young brother, Bernardo. He participated in some of the rehearsals but later dropped out, according to some sources because Dullin had refused to release him from his commitments at the Atelier, according to others because he had quarrelled with the star, Lady Abdy.

If the situation among the actors was not entirely happy, Artaud had shown immense flair in choosing his other collaborators. The great painter Balthus, whom Artaud deeply admired, agreed to design the scenery and costumes, and Roger Désormière composed the music, using up-to-date instruments like the Ondes Martenot. Artaud, who was convinced of the importance of sound in a production, was also in advance of his time in the use of prerecorded natural sounds coming stereophonically from loudspeakers placed in the auditorium: the bells of a cathedral (according to some Amiens, according to others Chartres) were used to great effect, as was real thunder, the noise of machinery, etc.

The opening night, a gala performance under the patronage of H.R.H. Prince George of Greece, the Princesse de Polignac, and other society leaders in aid of the Cercle François Villon, was on 6 May 1935. The elegant establishment figures mingled with intellectuals in their berets and made the ugly old theater with its hideously tasteless decoration vibrate with excitement. The reception seemed enthusiastic. But the reviews in the press were, on the whole, unfavorable. Far from being avant-garde, the melodramatic tragedy struck some critics as old-fashioned romantic fustian. And Lady Abdy, while admired for her grace and austere beauty, was savaged for her Russian accent and inaudible delivery. Others felt that Artaud would have been wiser to entrust the leading role to an actor less extreme and exaggerated than himself. He was accused of shouting his lines in paroxysms of intensity.

All now depended on the box-office. Would the public come? They did not. The play had to close, after seventeen performances, on 22 May.

For Artaud it was a catastrophe. This had been his last chance to establish himself as a working director in the theater of Paris. It had failed. No one would ever again be prepared to let him realize what were regarded as his extravagant and impractical ideas. This was more than merely a flop from which one could recover. It was, in effect, the end of Artaud's struggle since the early 1920s to find a basis for a normal existence within the framework of society as it was constituted. André Frank has movingly recalled Artaud during the last days of the run of *Les Cenci* when he first became aware of the significance of his failure:

> I remember a terrible evening in the theater when Antonin Artaud for the first time showed the cramped, "remote" face, cut off from the world, which has become the face by which we know him today. A financial failure, a chain of incomprehensions, had decided his fate: Artaud, the tragic genius, Artaud the prophet and magus, had come into existence.[9]

Jean-Louis Barrault offered Artaud the chance of collaborating with him on one of his theatrical ventures. But Artaud knew that it was too late. He declined the offer: "I no longer believe in being associated with others, particularly since my experience with surrealism, because I no longer believe in the purity of mankind" (*OC* v, 262).

[9] Ibid., p. 71.

What was he to do? He realized that he had reached
the end of one road. There would have to be something
like a new beginning. As far back as February he had
suggested to Paulhan that the *NRF* should publish a
volume of his collected writings on the theater. Yet
there was clearly no chance of his making a living as
a writer. He had had some success as a lecturer at the
Sorbonne. Perhaps he could lecture abroad. Filled with
disgust as he was at the corruption of French and
European society and art, yearning as he was for the
freshness and purity of extra-European cultures, Balinese, Chinese, Tibetan, he decided to try to leave Europe.
His health, in spite of repeated attempts to cure himself
of addiction, had been undermined by years of drug
taking. He wanted to abandon drugs and yet was passionately interested in them. Having worked on a project
to dramatize the Spanish conquest of Mexico, he had
become aware of the existence of a mystical cult based
on drugs there. All these considerations finally added up
to the idea that he should go to Mexico as an apostle of
French culture and, once there, study the remains of
pre-Columbian culture and the cult of peyotl.

Through Paulhan, who had contacts at the French
Ministry of Foreign Affairs, Artaud eventually succeeded in obtaining some sort of official approval for
his trip—a *titre de mission*—from the French Ministry
of Education. Although this was little more than a
formal endorsement, without any implication of financial subsidy, it at least had an effect on the Mexican
Legation in Paris, which also gave its blessing. And as
a result there was a chance that invitations to lecture
and commissions for articles would be forthcoming
once Artaud reached Mexico. To get there he had to
borrow from his friends: Barrault, Lise Deharme, Paulhan, and others advanced him some money and the
Compagnie Transatlantique agreed to give him a fifty
per cent reduction on his fare.

The last months of 1935 were spent in preparing for
this adventure. In the late autumn, shortly before his

departure, Artaud met a young Belgian girl, Cécile Schramme, and fell deeply in love with her. She made him yearn for health and appeared in some ways as an embodiment of his dream of a return to a more normal existence. And as the day of his departure drew nearer, he was also putting the finishing touches to the collection of essays about the theater which the *NRF* had undertaken to publish. Three days before he left Paris for Antwerp, on 6 January 1936, he sent Paulhan the suggested order in which the essays should be published. No title had yet been chosen for the book. It was during the sea voyage from Antwerp to Havana that he finally decided on a title and wrote to Paulhan about it: "I think I have found a suitable title for my book. It will be *The Theater and Its Double*. For if the theater is a double of life, life is a double of true theater. . . . The double of the theater is the *reality* which today's mankind leave unused" (*OC* v, 272-73).

The S.S. *Albertville* sailed from Antwerp on 10 January and arrived in Havana on 30 January 1936. It was Artaud's first glimpse of the New World. And here there happened something to which he later attached immense, cosmic importance: In circumstances which he regarded as mysterious and fateful he somehow obtained a small dagger or replica of a sword, a Toledan blade. It had, he maintained, been given him by a Negro sorcerer as a gift. He looked upon it as a powerful omen of good fortune to come.

On 7 February he disembarked on Mexican soil at Vera Cruz and took the train to Mexico City.

In Mexico he was well received as a prominent Frenchman, an established figure of Parisian cultural life who could speak with authority about latest developments in the world's artistic capital. He was lionized, invited to lunch by the French Minister, commissioned to write a series of articles for an important newspaper, *El Nacional Revolucionario*, and invited to lecture at various institutions of higher learning.

Yet it was not all smooth sailing. He was in constant

financial trouble. And he managed to offend some powerful circles. The Communist party, an important force in Mexican politics at the time, took umbrage at his disparaging remarks about the political commitment of the surrealists. Nor was his insistence on the inherent superiority of ancient Indian culture over the corrupt civilization of Europe wholly welcome to a regime which was desperately trying to drag Mexico into an industrial, twentieth-century way of life.

In spite of all this, he succeeded eventually in obtaining, with the help of the rector of Mexico University, financial assistance for a visit to an area inhabited by hitherto unspoiled Indian tribes to study their art. At the end of August 1936 he set out, by train, to cover the eight hundred miles to Chihuahua. From there, riding on a horse, he traveled into the Sierra Madre and into the country inhabited by the Tarahumara tribe, the Sierra Tarahumara. If we are to believe the description he gave of this ride after his return to Paris, it was a most painful journey: Two men had to lift him on and off the horse, so helpless and sick was Artaud; they had to put the reins into his hands and even close them around the reins, as he was unable to control his own movements. Perhaps this state of enfeeblement was due to the fact that he had abandoned the use of drugs in order to prepare his body to receive the peyotl. During the ride he had the impression that the rock formations resembled either the image of a dying man or female breasts, and he felt compelled to count the rocks, only to find that they recurred with miraculous regularity in groups of three, four, seven and eight. He was reminded of the music of numbers in the Cabbala.

When he arrived in the country of the Tarahumara, Artaud, who carried a letter from the Ministry of Education, was housed in the local school. The teacher aroused Artaud's dislike by obviously being eager to stamp out the last vestiges of the native religion, but also by being mainly preoccupied with fornicating with his female colleague. It was only after lengthy arguments that Artaud finally persuaded the teacher to allow the village priests to perform their ritual. He also apparently succeeded in obtaining some peyotl. After his return to Paris he recorded that it made him think "then, at that moment, that I was living through the happiest three days of my existence. I had ceased to be bored, to seek a reason for my existence, and I ceased to have to carry my body. I understood that I invented life, and that *that* was my function and my *raison d'être* and that I was bored when I no longer had my imagination and that the peyotl gave me imagination" (*OC* IX, 117).

By 7 October Artaud was back in Chihuahua and anxiously inquired from Paulhan whether *The Theater and Its Double* had yet appeared. He also announced that he was about to return to France. On 31 October he embarked on the *Mexique* and arrived back in France at St. Nazaire on 12 November.

The flight to the New World had proved a failure. It had not provided Artaud with a basis for an ordered existence. Back in Paris he was destitute, ravaged by drug addiction, without visible means of support. Jean-Marie Conty allowed him to stay in his house. Paulhan promised to publish his account of his journey into the land of the Tarahumara. Other friends helped him out with money. He met Cécile Schramme again, the Belgian girl who had so deeply impressed him before his departure for Mexico. His love letters to her between January and May 1937 give a pathetic picture of deep affection and a dream of married happiness, but also of continuous quarrels: Artaud wanted to reach the pinnacle of spiritual, nonsexual love and reproached Cécile with secret relapses into the common ways of female sexual greed. At the same time Artaud was resolved to purge himself of the drug habit. A grant of 600 francs, as an emergency subsidy, from the Ministry of Education's Caisse des Lettres enabled him to undergo a disintoxication treatment (25 February to 4 March 1937) at the Centre Français de Medicine et de Chirurgie in the Rue Boileau. But this did not succeed in ridding him of the aftereffects of long years of addiction to laudanum, opium, and heroin. From 14 to 29 April he made another effort, this time in a clinic at Sceaux. After this he felt much changed and able to meet his fiancée's parents, respectable bourgeois of Brussels.

On 18 May he was to deliver a lecture on the crisis of the cultural life of Paris, as seen by a traveler recently returned from Mexico, at the Brussels Maison de l'Art. It is difficult now to establish what actually happened at this occasion; it certainly ended in scandal. According to one account, Artaud announced that he would not be talking about the advertised subject and would instead give an account of his travels to the Tarahumara. As he was talking his attitude toward the audience became more and more aggressive and he ended with a furious shriek: "In revealing all this to you, I have probably killed myself." After which he remained motionless, with his eyes closed. According to rumors circulating in Brussels at the time, however, Artaud had shocked his audience by discussing, instead of his advertised subject, "the effects of masturbation on the Jesuits." While this is itself improbable, it shows the impression his behavior had made on at least some members of his audience.

On 21 May, back in Paris, Artaud was still writing to Paulhan asking him to act as best man at his marriage to Cécile Schramme. But, in fact, the engagement was already off. Cécile's parents, with whom Artaud had stayed at Brussels, were scandalized and far from satisfied that the strange Paris bohemian was a suitable husband for their daughter. Later Artaud bitterly complained that Cécile herself had been spreading calumnies about him, telling people that he was subject to fits of madness.

The disaster of the trip to Brussels was another turning point. Artaud became convinced that his very name had to disappear, an indication that he felt that his entire previous existence had collapsed. He begged Paulhan, at the beginning of June 1937, to publish his account of his trip to the Tarahumara anonymously, with merely three asterisks in place of the author's name. "Very soon I shall be dead or else in a situation . . . in which I shall not need a name. I am counting on you for the three asterisks" (*OC* vii, 227). The change he was expecting to undergo was connected with his increased preoccupation with magic and miraculous signs surrounding him. One of these was the mysterious little sword in Toledan steel that he had received from the sorcerer in Havana. But even more powerful and fateful was an Irish walking stick which his friend René Thomas had given him, and of which it was said that it might have belonged to St. Patrick himself, being perhaps the very stick with which he banished snakes from Ireland. Artaud, in any case, later maintained that this walking stick, "which everybody has been able to see in Paris in May, June, July, and August 1937," had been given to René Thomas by "the daughter of a Savoyard magician" (*OC* ix, 195). This cane had thirteen knobs or knots, and Artaud was convinced that this was the identical number of knots on St. Patrick's stick, of which, he remembered, he had read in a dictionary of hagiography he had consulted in the Bibliothèque Nationale in 1934 when researching his book on Heliogabalus.

To fathom the significance of all these magical events Artaud was taking lessons in the interpretation of the tarot pack. In June 1937 he experienced illumination. And as a result he published, at the end of July, a brochure, without an author's name and merely signed "Le Révélé" ("The Revealed One"), *Les Nouvelles Révélations de l'Etre* (*The New Revelations of Being*) in which he prophesied the forthcoming destruction of civilization by Fire, Water, Earth, and "a Star which will occupy the entire surface of the air, in which the Spirit of Man had been immersed" (*OC* VII, 173). It is a strange work, filled with numerological calculations and tarot interpretations, yet imbued with a powerful, poetic impetus of divine fury. It is also a declaration to the world that the author has reached a state of final separation from normal existence:

> I have struggled to try and exist, to try and consent to the forms (all the forms) with which the delirious illusion of being in the world has imbued reality.
>
> I no longer want to be deceived by illusions. Dead for the world; to that which for all others constitutes the world; fallen at last, fallen, risen into the void which I had rejected, I have a body which experiences the world and spews out reality.
>
> He who is speaking to you is one who has truly despaired and who has known the happiness of being in the world only now when he has left the world, when he is absolutely separated from it.
>
> Being dead, the others are not separated. They are still circling around their own corpses.
>
> I am not dead. But I am separated. (*OC* II, 150-51).

The miraculous little sword and the cane are variously referred to in the book: "I have the sword from an African Negro; the cane I have from God" (*OC* VII, 163). The male and female principle play a considerable part. One cycle of the world's history is approaching its end; it was dominated by the female principle, which stands for the Left, Republic, and Democracy. This means that the masses will again fall under the yoke. They deserve it. And through whom is this cosmic change to happen? "Through a Madman who is also a Sage and who sees himself as both Sage and Madman." This image recurs in various guises through the tarot symbols. "The tortured man has been taken for a Madman by everybody. He has appeared before the world as a Madman. And the image of the world's madness was incarnated in tortured man" (*OC* VII, 170). And that Artaud saw himself as the tortured man becomes clear at the end of the pamphlet in which he predicts the holocaust for November 1937:

> On the 7th [of November] the Destruction explodes in Lightning. The Tortured Man becomes, for the whole World, the Recognized One,
> The Revealed One (*OC* VII, 174)

In thus signing the pamphlet Artaud reveals *himself* as the tortured bringer of destruction—and through destruction, salvation—to the world.

Convinced that destiny called him to a cosmic event, Artaud felt that he had to be in the right place when it occurred. And that right place was the country where his miraculous walking stick had come from—the West of Ireland, the country of St. Patrick.

So, following the same instinct that had driven him to Mexico, but in a state far less lucid, far more exalted, Artaud prepared himself for another journey into the unknown. Having lost Cécile Schramme he developed new fervent attachments to women; he saw a mystic bond between himself and Jacqueline Breton, André Breton's daughter. (After his return from Mexico he had renewed his old friendship with Breton and buried the old clamorous feuds with him.) Another woman who began to play an important part in his life and to whom he addressed passionate letters was Anne Manson, a young journalist who, planning a trip to Mexico, had been advised to contact Artaud. It was to these women he poured out his visions, warning them of the dangers of future destruction and promising them his protection. And his behavior became ever more strange. In August 1937 Anaïs Nin noted in her diary: "The Dôme at nine in the morning. Antonin Artaud passes by. He is waving his magic Mexican cane and shouting."[10]

On 14 August Artaud sent his first postcards from

[10] *The Diary of Anaïs Nin*, Vol. II, p. 247.

Ireland to René Thomas, who had given him the magic cane (which Anaïs Nin had, understandably, mistaken for a Mexican object), his sister, and André Breton. He had arrived at Cobh. On 17 August he was in Galway. On 23 August he wrote to Anne Manson from the island of Inishmore in the Aran Islands, where he had found lodgings in a remote village, more than two hours' walk from the nearest post office at Kilronan. He had run out of money by then and was asking Breton and Paulhan to help him. On 2 September he left the island (apparently without paying his bill at the place where he had stayed) and went to Galway where he took lodgings at the Imperial Hotel. A letter he wrote to Breton from there on 5 September was, he declared, the last he would ever sign with his name; henceforth he would be known by another name. On 8 September he left Galway, apparently for Dublin. As the hour of the catastrophe he had foreseen for the world approached, the miraculous cane changed character: On 14 September he wrote to Anne Manson, "I hold Jesus Christ's own baton and it is Jesus Christ who commands me, and all that I shall do; and it will be seen that His teaching was for Metaphysical Heroes and not for idiots" (OC VII, 282). But in a letter to Breton written on the same day he made it clear that the Jesus Christ whose cane he possessed had nothing to do with the Jesus Christ of Christianity. If the Holy Ghost was a force urging men to live, Artaud's Christ-Shiva called men toward the Absolute, because he recognized that life is evil and death the ultimate good.

What actually happened to Artaud in Dublin in late September 1937 remains shrouded in mystery. The most probable version is that, completely without money and in considerable distress, he tried to make contact with some religious house which he thought might contain French-speaking monks. It is said that, having tried to gain access to a monastery (or perhaps even a convent) late at night and not getting anyone to open the door, he made such a noise in the street that the police were called to put an end to the disturbance. As he resisted being moved on, there was a scuffle in which the miraculous cane of St. Patrick was lost. He spent six days in detention and was finally put on a ship bound for Le Havre, the S.S. *Washington,* which left Cobh on 29 September.

Worse was to come. Having been assigned a cabin on board the *Washington,* Artaud, it seems, was alarmed by the sudden appearance of a steward and a mechanic, carrying metal implements, probably in order to repair a washbasin. Convinced that the two sinister figures had come to harm him, Artaud furiously attacked them and had to be overpowered and put into a straitjacket. On arrival at Le Havre the next day the owners of the ship handed him over to the French authorities, who promptly interned him in an asylum as a dangerous lunatic. It was the beginning of nine long years of confinement in mental institutions.

Artaud had predicted the ultimate catastrophe for November 1937. As far as the ultimate catastrophe for himself was concerned, his margin of error amounted to barely more than a month. And with regard to the whole world's holocaust—the outbreak of the Second World War—that occurred within less than two years of the predicted date. Detained first in Le Havre, then transferred to the asylum of Quatre-Mares at Sotteville-lès-Rouen, Artaud had disappeared from the view of all his friends. Artaud's mother had been notified by the shipping line of her son's internment, but had some difficulty in discovering his whereabouts. She finally traced him to Quatre-Mares but he was unable to recognize her. Whatever his mental state might have been at the moment when, unable to communicate in a world which did not speak his language, he had suddenly been overpowered and detained, the shock of this sudden incarceration would, in itself, more than account for his having fallen into an almost catatonic state.

His family desperately tried to have him freed, or at

least moved nearer to Paris, where it would be easier to visit him. On 12 April 1938 these efforts resulted in his transfer to the mental hospital of Sainte-Anne in Paris. Here some of his friends were able to gain access to him, but he hardly responded. In fact, the authorities came to the conclusion that he was incurable; he was accordingly transferred to an institution for such cases, the mental hospital of Ville Evrard on the outskirts of Paris, on 27 February 1939.

It is ironical that, at the very moment when Artaud was in a near-catatonic state in the hospital of Sainte-Anne, the book through which he still exercises a deep influence on the development of the theater, *The Theater and Its Double*, was finally published. He had collected the articles and essays it contains before his departure to Mexico, had begged Paulhan to speed its publication before leaving for Ireland, and had asked for an advance for it while penniless in the Aran Islands. At last, in February 1938, it appeared in the Gallimard series *Métamorphoses* in an edition limited to four hundred copies—and its author was not even aware of it.

Yet the publication had drawn attention to Artaud and interest in him reawakened among the intellectuals of Paris. From Ville Evrard Artaud also began to remind his friends of his existence. He started writing letters and agreed to see visitors. "I am a fanatic, I am not a madman," he wrote to Jacqueline Breton on 7 April 1939. To Roger Blin and Charles Dullin he addressed moving appeals to rescue him from confinement. At the end of 1940 he began to write again to Genica Athanasiou, the companion of his early years in Paris. He knew, he said, that she had fought valiantly in the battles conducted by his friends for his release. (He later told Breton that tens of thousands had filled the streets of Le Havre demanding his release at the moment of his arrest and that Breton had, in fact, been killed during the ensuing massacre.) "Heroin must be procured at all costs and it must be brought to me even at the risk of getting killed. . . . The initiates have real instruments of torture, as I have told you, and they use them from afar to mutilate me a little more every night while I am asleep," he wrote to Genica on 24 November 1940. "Genica, we must leave this world, but to be able to do that, the Reign of the Other World must come, and for that armed troops in great numbers are needed. So that the Bohemians can enter *in numbers* into this world, as one passes from a ship to the quayside, I need heroin to open the hidden doors for them and to break the spells of Satan which keep them out and me prisoner here."[11]

There is no doubt that Artaud's rage at being confined also led him into violent fantasies of persecution. According to Jean-Louis Brau, a series of letters written by Artaud to one of the doctors at the asylum, which are extant, cannot as yet be published because of the most terrible accusations they contain against persons who are still alive.

As time passed and Artaud remained at Ville Evrard, the situation became more and more dangerous for him. France, by then, was under German occupation. There was a severe shortage of food; the inmates of lunatic asylums were at the very bottom of the list of priorities. Moreover it was known that, in Germany itself, lunatics and mental defectives had been liquidated by the authorities´ to save food supplies. Artaud's mother and those of his friends who occasionally visited him were appalled by his loss of weight and his emaciated state.

Desnos, Eluard, Barrault, Theodore Fraenkel, and Arthur Adamov were trying to think of ways and means to save Artaud. Mme. Bourdet, a cousin of Adamov's, had been impressed by the humanity and openness of mind of a psychiatrist, Dr. Gaston Ferdière, whom she had met while he was in charge of an institution near where she lived and who had since then become head of

11 *Lettres à Genica Athanasiou*, pp. 309-310.

a mental hospital in the south of France, in the zone then still unoccupied by the Germans where conditions were much easier. Ferdière, himself a poet and essayist of some note, had frequented the intellectual circles where Artaud had moved in the 1930s and may even have met him occasionally. He was certainly aware of Artaud's stature as a poet and man of the theater. When Desnos approached Ferdière in November 1942, he readily agreed to do his best for Artaud and to take him into his institution at Rodez, some one hundred miles northeast of Toulouse. But to transfer a mental patient across the zonal borders was far from easy. Ferdière hit upon a solution: Desnos and Artaud's family would ask for his transfer to another institution *within* the German zone of occupation, but very near the demarcation line, the "rural" mental asylum at Chézal-Benoît, of which Ferdière had previously been the medical director, and where he still had friends willing to help him. From there it would be easier to move Artaud across the demarcation line. Desnos managed to obtain permission to have Artaud moved from Ville Evrard in January 1943. On the eve of his departure he went to visit him and, not having seen him for five years, was horrified to find him emaciated and in a state of delirium, "talking like St. Jerome and unwilling to leave because it might remove him from the magical powers at work for him."[12] Nevertheless Desnos persuaded Artaud's mother to give her permission to have her son moved.

Artaud left Ville Evrard on 22 January and, after spending three weeks at Chézal-Benoît, arrived at Rodez in the early morning of 11 February. Ferdière went to meet Artaud at the station. He was, so he later said, determined from the beginning to treat him with the respect due to a great poet, however sick he might be. Artaud declared himself happy to meet him again and

[12] *La Tour de Feu*, No. 63-64, p. 31.

although Ferdière, who had seen him from the distance, could not remember actually having been introduced to him, he readily responded. "I said, 'Yes, certainly I remember, I'm glad you've come here,' and very soon I was treating Artaud not as a sick man withdrawn from the world but as someone I knew intimately; and I tried to restore to him the quality of human dignity of which he had been so long deprived. My wife helped me to play this little game . . . so when we arrived at Rodez, she immediately invited him to lunch."[13] Fréderic Delanglade, a painter who was a friend of Ferdière's, was present at this lunch. Artaud, when introduced by his name, retorted: "Antonin Artaud is dead, my name is Antonin Nalpas."[14] Until September 1943 he continued to sign his letters with that—his mother's maiden—name.

Although Artaud behaved extremely strangely, uttering wild cries and circling about the room, Ferdière treated him as a friend, gave him a small room of his own, and, as the Aveyron department was in a fertile region and had a flourishing black market, fattened him up with milk, honey, biscuits, and other foods he had not tasted for years.

When he arrived at Rodez Artaud had already spent almost five and a half years in mental institutions. At Rodez he began a copious correspondence with numerous old friends and acquaintances and also wrote long letters to the doctors at Rodez. These reveal that he had become extremely pious and eager to attend church services. He attributed his internment to the machinations of the Antichrist and his agents, the French police, who were in league with the Jews and other sinister forces of evil. They had poisoned him and were keeping from him the only antidote to the poison from which he suffered—and that antidote was opium. The poison which

---

[13] Ferdière, in BBC broadcast.
[14] *La Tour de Feu,* p. 75.

was the cause of Artaud's torments, however, was sperm, obtained by the police by putting vast crowds of people under erotic spells which induced them into ritual masturbation.

> All sexuality and all eroticism . . . are a sin and a crime against Jesus Christ and the antidote to eroticism and the spells of the Demon is opium and it is to prevent me from taking opium and to leave me as a target for the erotic maneuvers of the demons against me that the French police, which entirely belongs to the Antichrist, is keeping me prisoner. To cure me of Evil I need opium and to refuse me opium amounts to becoming an accomplice of the Demons. (OC x, 16).

Antonin Artaud, he claimed in another letter, had died at Ville Evrard in August 1939; it was merely his body which had remained as a vessel into which God would descend when it was duly purified (OC x, 40). In a letter to Paulhan dated 7 July 1943, he spoke of Saint-Artaud, who had dominated vast crowds trying to prevent him from going to Ireland by striking lightning from St. Patrick's cane outside the offices of the NRF in the Rue Sébastien Bottin; and that he had gone to Ireland to return the sacred cane of St. Patrick to St. Patrick's Cathedral in Dublin, where it had been attached to a wall for fifteen thousand years until it disappeared in the nineteenth century; and that, while in Dublin he had also ascertained that the Holy Grail, which had been brought to Ireland by King Cormac Mac Art, was still there. And if Antonin Artaud had led a double life, so did Jean Paulhan, who was also known in paradise and among the saints as Dionysos the Aeropagite (OC x, 57-59). The idea that several different souls could successively inhabit the same body dominated much of Artaud's thought at this period. Of friends who somehow disappointed him he maintained that they had died, while some demon continued to inhabit their bodies and deceived all those with whom they came into contact into thinking that they were still alive.

Another dominant idea of his fantasies at this time was the utter wickedness of all sexuality. In a long letter to one of the doctors at Rodez Artaud argued that God had created man without the need of sexual reproduction or defecation. Originally man possessed neither sexual nor digestive organs; food was originally eliminated by "lumbar evaporation." It was Antichrist who had seduced man into the filthy habits of coition and digestion (*OC* x, 31-35).

The body of Antonin Artaud had, he asserted again and again, carried all the world's sins and impurities; that was the reason for his intense suffering. Artaud's soul, on the other hand, he told Jean-Louis Barrault in one of his early letters from Rodez, was that of an angel who had previously dwelt on earth under the name of St. Hyppolitus, Bishop of Piraeus in the second century A.D. (*OC* x, 40). Yet he frequently heard other people converse within his own body, he told Frédéric Delanglade, "because my thoughts are pure, and, when I have a bad thought, I never believe that it is my own and immediately try to discover the impure consciousness which has sent it to soil me" (*OC* x, 52).

Dr. Ferdière tried to stimulate Artaud into activity, encouraging him to draw, lending him books, and later suggesting that he should make translations from the English. In the course of 1944 Artaud translated Robert Southwell's *The Burning Babe*, which Pierre Seghers published in *Poésie 44*, Edgar Allan Poe's *Israfel*, and Lewis Carroll's *Ye Carpette Knight* (although Artaud had always detested Lewis Carroll). As early as the autumn of 1943 a publisher, Robert J. Godet, approached Artaud for permission to publish the texts about his voyage to Mexico, which had appeared in the *NRF* before the war, as an illustrated book. Ferdière encouraged Artaud to write additional material about his

Mexican adventure and Artaud immediately set to work on the first of several essays, which, although the original plan of publication came to nothing, eventually appeared in book form.

Occupational therapy was not the only form of treatment Ferdière had in store for Artaud. He felt that Artaud was in danger of further deterioration and of a gradual but continuous slide into ever deeper alienation, delusion, and eventual apathy. And so he decided to subject him to several courses of electric shock treatment. For Artaud this amounted to sheer torture and later became the subject of bitter accusations against Ferdière from Artaud and his supporters. For although, as Ferdière never tired of pointing out, the actual treatment is painless, Artaud was filled with horror and fear of the moment when, on regaining consciousness, the patient is at first unaware of his whereabouts and, indeed, his own identity. These moments of reawakening into a void caused Artaud profound existential anguish. By July 1945, after two years at Rodez, Artaud maintained that he had been through no less than fifty such comas (OC x, 93). On the other hand, Ferdière claimed that the electric shock treatment was greatly improving Artaud's behavior and was dispelling his obsessions and delusions. There were certainly indications of an improvement in Artaud's state of mind. In a letter addressed to one of the doctors at Rodez who had been against continuing the shock treatment, Artaud pleaded with him to stop any further such torture, on the grounds that "I no longer believe in the demons of hell as I did two years ago when I arrived here. . . . And as I don't want to think of these any more I have, for quite a long time now, stopped seeing anything but the paper on which I am writing, the people, the trees, the houses among which I live, and the blue sky above (OC xi, 14). Was this new attitude—from which Artaud quite soon relapsed into further accusations against "initiates" who were poisoning him and keeping him under their spell—the result of the treatment? Or did it merely show that in his fear of further torture Artaud was prepared to assert anything which he believed might convince his tormentors that he no longer needed electric shock treatment?

Be that as it may, by the spring of 1945 Artaud had emerged from his lengthy period of religious fervor. It was, he told Blin in a letter, in April, on Passion Sunday, that he had "thrown communion, the Eucharist, God and his Christ out of the window and I have decided to be myself, that is, simply Antonin Artaud, a religious unbeliever by nature and soul who has never hated anything more than God and his religions, whether that of Christ or Jehovah or Brahma, not forgetting the naturist rites of the lamas" (*OC* XI, 29). Yet in the same letter he insisted that he was under more spells than ever and that the Sûreté Générale, the British Intelligence service, and the Vatican's Congregation of the Index were plotting against him.

In May 1944 *The Theater and Its Double* had been reissued by Gallimard. And after the liberation of Paris in August of that year, as literary life gradually returned to normality, Artaud was able to resume contact with his former literary circle and to make the acquaintance of a new generation for whom he had become something of a legendary, martyred figure. He was greatly touched when a young writer and critic, Henri Thomas, who was writing an essay on the *Theater and Its Double*, approached him in January 1945 with a request for personal information and permission to visit him. Ironically, at that time Artaud himself had not yet seen his book. When at last a copy of the new edition reached him at the end of January, the first he had ever held in his hand, he wrote to Paulhan: "My heart is deeply agitated to see so much dynamism, such forcefulness of style at the service of ideas which, in the face of the upheaval, the disorder, the anarchy and war of the present situation, no longer are directed at the points that should be aimed at" (*OC* XI, 29). By now Artaud was no longer confined within the asylum; he was able to go for walks around Rodez, a little town with a fine cathedral. And he received more and more visitors from Paris: Raymond Queneau had come to see him as early as Christmas 1943. After the end of the war Jean Dubuffet, Henri Thomas, and others came to Rodez, were horrified by the dinginess of the asylum in its ancient building, and strolled through the town in deep conversation with Artaud.

Among the new friends with whom Artaud corresponded after the liberation was Henri Parisot, a young man who was trying to relaunch the project, which had become bogged down, of a book about Artaud's visit to Mexico. When Parisot suggested that he might publish the five long letters he had received from Artaud in the autumn of 1945 and which gave an account of his views about the origins of his confinement, his drug addiction, and language, poetry, and art, Artaud agreed. When that little book, the *Letters from Rodez*, appeared in April 1946, Artaud was already on the eve of his departure from the asylum.

Artaud's former friends and the growing number of new admirers had long been trying to free him from his confinement: Early in 1946 Marthe Robert, the translator of Kafka, and Arthur Adamov came to Rodez to negotiate with Dr. Ferdière about Artaud's release. Ferdière agreed on condition that he should be satisfied that Artaud's livelihood was assured. Accordingly a committee was formed in Paris with the task of raising sufficient funds.

The committee's appeal for help found a most generous response. Artists like Picasso, Giacometti, Duchamp, Braque, Arp, Léger, Masson, to name but a few of the most famous, donated works to be sold at auction, together with manuscripts and autographs provided by writers of the stature of Gide, Eluard, Mauriac, Sartre, René Char, Supervielle, and Tzara; while Artaud's theatrical friends were planning a gala matinée with the participation of Barrault, Blin, Dullin, Jouvet, Alain Cuny, and Jean Vilar. Ferdière was satisfied. He released Artaud from the asylum on 19 March 1946, but advised him to spend some time on his own in a village some twenty kilometers from Rodez. He returned to Rodez on 14 April and was accompanied by Ferdière himself to Paris on 26 May 1946.

On the platform of the Gare d'Austerlitz a group of Artaud's friends was waiting for the arrival of the night train from Rodez. The man they welcomed back to the city he had left almost nine years earlier was not yet fifty. But toothless, wrinkled, ravaged as he was, he looked well over seventy. Ferdière had recommended that Artaud should remain under some psychiatric care. So his friends had arranged for him to lodge, as a purely voluntary patient, in an old pavilion in the garden of the psychiatric hospital at Ivry, on the outskirts of Paris, near the endpoint of the metroline which goes to the Mairie d'Ivry. Gérard de Nerval, one of the *poètes maudits* with whom Artaud felt so much kinship, had been an inmate of that same institution, and Artaud also maintained that some of the heroes of the French Revolution, Robespierre and Màrat, had made speeches in the building.

The auction of works of art, which opened with a *vernissage* at the Galerie Pierre (managed by Pierre Loeb) on 6 June, and the benefit performance at the Théâtre Sarah-Bernhardt at 5 p.m. on 7 June were a great success and realized the sum of about a million (postwar inflated) francs for Artaud. The matinée at the theater was attended by *tout Paris*: Vilar, Cuny, Jouvet, and Rouleau read from Artaud's works; Colette Thomas, Henri Thomas's wife, recited a recent poem she had rehearsed with Artaud himself; this was Artaud's authentic voice and the outstanding performance of the evening. Breton, Dullin, Adamov, and Barrault spoke about Artaud. Then Barrault announced that there would be a reading from *Les Cenci* lasting forty minutes. The young poet Jacques Prevel, one of those who had written to Artaud at Rodez, noted in his diary that Barrault gave a tremendous performance. Strangely enough, Barrault himself has subsequently denied any recollection of having taken part in this benefit performance, although his name is on the advertisement for it and although witnesses like Prevel have recorded the fact. The reason may well be that Barrault, who later became disgusted by the cult of Artaud in circles he disliked, simply does not want to remember.

Artaud himself was not present in the theater. He waited at a café for the performance to end and then happily wandered off with Adamov.

Back in the familiar and yet now so different world of the cafés of St. Germain-des-Prés, surrounded by old friends and new admirers, Artaud became immensely active: He who had had such difficulty in putting his thoughts on paper was now writing incessantly, day and night, at home, with friends in cafés, on the metro; the barriers which had stood between his thought and its expression and which he had so movingly described in the correspondence with Rivière had fallen, and when existing words failed him, he inserted newly formed words as yet without meaning or simply random groups of vowels and consonants which stood for inarticulate cries and murmurs.

Gallimard planned an edition of his complete works. For this he wrote a *Preamble* in which he affirmed that he had abandoned the search for perfect expression: "Whether my sentences sound French or Papuan, that's exactly what I don't care a damn." He also added, as supplements to the letters he had written to the Pope and the Dalai Lama in his surrealist period, new letters to these personages in which he used far more violent language and indeed, as far as the Dalai Lama was concerned, completely reversed his position. To the Pope he declared, among other things, that "it was I (not Jesus Christ) who was crucified on Golgatha; and I was crucified for having risen against God and his Christ, because I am a man and God and his Christ are only ideas, which, incidentally, carry the filthy marks of the hands of man; and these ideas have never existed for me" (*OC* 1, 17), while he accused the Dalai Lama and his like of being "merely filthy Europeans, after all, as the real Orient was nordic. . . . It is you who are the cause of the syllogism, of logic, of hysterical mysticism, of the dialectic" (*OC* 1, 23), to mention only a few of the crimes laid at his feet. While still in Rodez Artaud had planned a third mystical journey, this time to Tibet. Now, after his return to Paris, he was, as Prevel noted in his diary, thinking of it again. Speaking of the journey he planned to the Far East right into China, he said, "We'll go, fifty strong, armed with rifles and machine guns, and we'll settle some accounts with certain people, particularly in Tibet."[15]

Many of Artaud's poems written at this time immediately appeared in reviews or were issued as expensive pamphlets.

At the end of 1946 Artaud decided that he wanted to give a public reading of some of his current work. It was arranged that this should take place on 13 January 1947 at the Théâtre du Vieux Colombier. He was to read three poems, *Le Retour d'Artaud-le-Momo* ("momo" is Marseilles argot for a fool) among them. On 11 January he told Prevel that he was suffering from an eczema on his testicles, but that Dr. Thévenin, the husband of Paule Thévenin, who had become Artaud's unofficial secretary and helper (and later the editor of his collected works), had treated it and given him permission to appear.

The theater was sold out. The *Letters from Rodez* had made Artaud well known among the younger intellec-

---

[15] Jacques Prevel, *En compagnie d'Antonin Artaud*, p. 113.

tuals. But older literary figures like André Gide were also in the audience. Artaud, as he had done at the disastrous lecture in Brussels which had spoiled his chances of marriage, soon abandoned his prepared program and launched into an account of his sufferings at the hands of psychiatrists and of the horrors of electric shock treatment. Having dropped the papers with his prepared text, he went on talking for two hours; then his voice gave out. He stopped, and finally fled from the stage. André Gide felt that it was one of the most moving moments he had ever experienced: "Of his material being nothing remained except what was expressive."[16] But the paying customers on the whole felt let down and, to them, this appearance of Artaud in public, like so many previous ones, seemed nothing short of scandalous.

At about the same time, in January 1947, a great van Gogh exhibition was held at the Orangerie. Artaud went to see it and was overwhelmed by the work of a kindred spirit who had also languished in a lunatic asylum. When Pierre Loeb, the art dealer, a few days later showed Artaud an article in a newspaper which described van Gogh as a degenerate, Artaud became so incensed that he began writing an essay in defense of the painter. *Van Gogh, le suicidé de la société* is one of Artaud's most brilliant and influential works. It was awarded the Prix St. Beuve shortly after it appeared at the end of 1947. Apart from passages of splendid analysis and description of van Gogh's paintings, the essay is, above all, a furious polemic against psychiatrists and psychiatry. Part of it was published in an English translation by Peter Watson in the January 1948 *Horizon*. That is where R. D. Laing read it as a young student; he has since said that it came as a revelation to him and played a decisive part in his development.

[16] André Gide in *Combat*, 19 March 1948, in Jean-Louis Brau, *Antonin Artaud*, p. 235.

In July 1947 Pierre Loeb arranged an exhibition of Artaud's drawings at his gallery and Artaud also gave a reading of his poems there.

With several publications of his poems imminent (*Artaud-le-Momo* and *Ci-gît*), Artaud was much in demand. In November 1947 Fernand Pouey, in charge of literary and dramatic broadcasts at the French Radio, asked Artaud to appear in a series called *La Voix des poètes*. Using some of his writings which were already in existence (he asked Paule Thévenin to take part and to choose which of his texts she wanted to read), Artaud dictated a good deal of new material to form part of the broadcast, which he called *Pour en finir avec le jugement de Dieu*. The transmission was rehearsed and recorded from 22 to 29 November 1947 in the studios of the Radiodiffusion Française. Apart from Artaud the speakers were Paule Thévenin, Roger Blin, and Maria Casarès. Artaud himself accompanied some of the text on xylophone, drums, gongs, and other percussion instruments which were put at his disposal. After the program had been edited, in January 1948, Artaud made some cuts and even re-recorded part of it. The transmission was scheduled for 10:45 p.m. on 2 February. But on 1 February Wladimir Porché, the Director General of the Radiodiffusion Française, decided to cancel the broadcast.

Artaud certainly had produced some inflammatory material. The first text, which he spoke himself, concerned a plan he imagined he had heard about, according to which the United States, afraid that they would be lacking cannon-fodder for future wars they had planned, were stockpiling in deep-frozen form the sperm of little boys about to enter school, to be used in artificial insemination for the subsequent production of soldiers. In another passage God was called no more than shit, and ridicule was heaped on the Mass as well as on Jesus Christ. Pouey, the originator of the transmission, argued that had Rimbaud been alive he would probably have produced equally shocking material—and would posterity not have ridiculed broadcasting authorities that denied him the opportunity to be heard? The press was puzzled and outraged by the cancellation. As a result it was decided that the recording should be heard by a jury of prominent literary figures who could support Fernand Pouey in his resolve to have the program broadcast. This audition took place on 5 February: Among those who heard Artaud's poems were Raymond Queneau, Max-Pol Fouchet, Cocteau, Roger Vitrac, and other prominent personalities. They unanimously supported a broadcast. But the Director General remained adamant. Fernand Pouey resigned. The controversy in the press raged for many days. Again Artaud was at the center of a scandal and a storm. It was the last time.

Ever since he had arrived back in Paris Artaud had been in constant pursuit of drugs. He cadged laudanum wherever he could get it. Prevel's diary contains accounts of many incidents in which Artaud pleaded and begged for relief. He was in great pain. As it later turned out he was suffering from cancer of the anus. When his doctors allowed him as much chloral as he wanted, Artaud realized that he was doomed. One month after the final rejection of his broadcast, on the morning of 4 March 1948, he was found dead, sitting upright at the foot of his bed in his pavilion in the mental hospital of Ivry.

Roger Blin has given an account of how his friends kept vigil for three days and nights by his corpse in the little room, not because they believed in such ritual, but to keep away the rats, which infested the room by night, and the priests whom they were afraid Artaud's family might send to give him a religious funeral after all.

To the funeral, without religious rites, at the cemetery of Ivry, the mourners came in two distinct groups: One was formed by Artaud's family, the other by the friends and followers of his last twenty months in Paris. The feud between the family and the disciples continued for a long time. The family, who had inherited the copyright of Artaud's works, accused the friends of his last period of holding on to drawings and manuscripts which soon became extremely valuable; the disciples reproached the family with heartlessness and greed and a lack of understanding of their son's and brother's work. The publication of Artaud's complete works was delayed for many years by this acrimonious dispute.

Seen in retrospect Artaud's life falls into a pattern and becomes, as he himself so often proclaimed, his supreme work of art. There is an inner logic and consistency in his creation of his youthful image in films like *La Passion de Jeanne d'Arc* to provide a stunning and heart-rending contrast with that of the wizened martyr of society's rejection and contempt which became the image of his final epiphany. And there is a similar deep inner consistency in his gradual abandonment of the conventional objectives of the artist in pursuit of public recognition and fame, the discovery of himself as his supreme subject matter in the correspondence with Rivière, his brief adherence to surrealism, and his final apogee as the poet of utter spontaneity, scattering along his way writings which are no longer craftily wrought artifacts but bleeding pieces of flesh torn from his living, suffering body. There is even a satisfying meaningfulness in Artaud, the man of the theater, kept out of the promised land of rebirth and renewal but, like Moses, proclaiming its future laws while glimpsing it from afar, a tragic prophet. But, above all, there is perfection of design in his final descent into madness (if madness it should be called rather than a plumbing of the ultimate depths of human suffering and existential anguish): What else could he have done after the failure of his last theatrical venture, how else could he have lived through the war and occupation, how else could he, at the end, have emerged as the admired lodestar of a new generation? He had rejected abstract thought and proclaimed the supremacy of concrete experience and, by the pattern of his living, had incarnated his own conception of ar 's life and life as suffering.

The Limits of Language
● ● ●

iii

You say you are incapable of expressing your thought. How then do you explain the lucidity and brilliance with which you are expressing the thought that you are incapable of thought? That, in effect, was the paradox with which Rivière confronted Artaud in their correspondence.

The answer is simple enough: There is a vast difference between a *negative* statement, the bare acknowledgment of the fact that something is *not* there, on the one hand, and the *positive* assertion, on the other, that something is present, coupled with an accurate and exhaustive description of its nature, a description capable of fully conveying its quality. That Artaud was able to speak with eloquence about his inability to express his thoughts showed that he possessed the technical qualifications to express thought. Perhaps—and this was implied in Rivière's side of the correspondence—perhaps he had simply nothing, or too little, to say. All thought, after all, it could be argued, is verbal, is language; a thought incapable of being formulated in words therefore by definition would not be a thought, would not exist at all. Artaud had written his poems down; that was what he had had to say and he had said it. If these poems were judged not good enough for publication, how could he claim that the thought he had wanted to express had been better than the expression it had found in his poems?

To what extent can thought exist that is not formulated in words, that stubbornly resists being put into words at all? Are thought and language necessarily co-terminous? Artaud stubbornly persisted in bridging the chasm which seemed to open between his wordless poetic intuitions and their expression in language: "I am imbecile, through suppression of my thought, by the malformation of my thought, I am vacant through the paralysis of my tongue" (*OC* I, 116). Artaud was, at that period of his life, deeply conscious of this possibility. He experienced it as an inner void, a loss of the sense that he existed at all, and in a rage of deep frustration. In an early sketch for a silent film scenario, *Les dix-huit secondes* (*Eighteen Seconds*), the hero is a young actor,

who has been struck by a strange disease. He has become incapable of catching his thought; he has retained his entire lucidity; but whatever thought occurs to him, he is incapable of giving it external form, that is to translate it into the appropriate gestures or words. He lacks the words, they no longer respond to his call, he is reduced to seeing images pass inside him, a surfeit of contradictory images, unrelated among themselves. This makes him incapable of mingling with the lives of others or of pursuing any activity. (*OC* III, 12)

It was precisely because Artaud knew that he was suffering from a nervous disease that he persevered in trying to find a solution to the problem, remained convinced that his difficulty in formulating the positive content of his inner world was real and that thought *could* exist in an unformulated, preverbal state; and that it should be possible to find ways and means to bridge the gap between this amorphous, as yet uncreated thought and its expression. Indeed, in the period immediately after the correspondence with Rivière he felt that he had stumbled on a problem of great general importance for the understanding of the process of artistic creation itself. He still saw his condition as a disease, but a disease which, if studied as an extreme particular case of a general condition, could throw light on much more than one pathological instance. Again and again he attempted to analyze his condition and reached increasing refinement in describing it.

> If it is understood that any idea or image which arises in the unconscious and, through the intervention of the will, is to become a word in the mind, the question then is to find out at what point of its formation the gap opens up, and if, indeed, the manifestation of the will itself is a cause of the trouble, an occasion for that rupture; and whether the rupture occurs at this particular thought or the one which follows. (*OC* 1 Suppl., 140)

It might even be, he argued in this letter to George Soulié de Morant, one of the earliest European experts on Chinese acupuncture who was treating him at the time, that it was the very intensity and rapidity of the as yet unformulated thought which caused the blockage, manifested externally by his starting to stutter. But then, he continued, it might also be the case that language itself was inadequate to convey what he actually felt:

> If it is cold, I am still able to say that it is cold; but it may also happen that I am incapable of saying it: That is a fact, for there is inside me something wrong from the affective point of view, and if I am asked why I cannot say it, I shall reply that my internal

feeling on this fragmentary and insignificant matter simply does not correspond to the three simple little words which I should then have to utter. (*OC* i Suppl., 140)

This assertion had far-reaching implications: Perhaps it was not that Artaud was deficient in his inability to express his feelings and turn them into "thoughts," words, language; perhaps it was language itself which was incapable of expressing them adequately.

During the 1930s, the period when he was evolving his theory of theater, Artaud became more and more aware of such limitations of language. Having himself experienced the extreme difficulty of finding adequate expression for his ideas and feelings—his thought—he became increasingly contemptuous of writers and other artists using words (such as actors and directors) who seemed to be free of his difficulty. Rightly or wrongly, he attributed the ease with which they used language to intellectual laziness and a lack of integrity. Instead of struggling for expression in suffering and torment, as was his lot, they seemed simply to use ready-made formulations which they merely permutated in an endless series of facile rearrangements. Words, in their hands, had become a paper currency without backing, conventionalized tokens that had lost all contact with the reality they had once sprung from and were still deemed to represent.

The surrealist experiment had been one of the ways in which Artaud had tried to renew the potential of language and to break with conventionalized forms of literary expression: By letting the subconscious itself speak directly and without the intervention of the will, rationality, the awareness of the rules of grammar and rules of elegance of literary form, the surrealists, and Artaud with them, hoped to widen the potential of language, to make it capable of communicating the actual movement of emotion and the full range of the hidden treasures of human imagination.

Yet Artaud himself did not produce much poetry of significance during his surrealist period. He was still too preoccupied with his own case, too intent on analyzing his disability. It was this disability which led him toward a poetry that did not have to rely on language and could largely do without it—the theater.

Artaud was not a systematic thinker and never formulated his views on language in a fully developed theory. Yet it is possible to reconstruct the pattern of his thought on the subject.

Basically this amounts to the conviction that it was a profound mistake to equate all human consciousness with that part of it capable of verbal expression. Our consciousness is made up of a multitude of elements only a few of which are capable of being directly formulated in words. What we see with our eyes, for example, is constantly within our consciousness, yet is very rarely actually put into words or thought about verbally. The same applies to visual memories, or internally visualized wish-fulfillment, daydreaming. There are the many *sounds* which surround us or drift through our imagination. There are the smells impinging upon us, of which we may hardly be conscious because they form a constant background to our lives, but which, at times, are capable of evoking the most powerful associations and memories (one only has to think of Proust's famous *madeleine*). But, above all, there are the numerous body sensations which are constantly felt although they are hardly ever converted into verbal form: the pressure of the clothes we wear upon our skin, the movement of the air in the room, and other external influences, as well as those which operate from within us—the rhythm of our heartbeat and our breathing, the tension of our muscles, the fullness or emptiness of our stomachs, etc.

All these are at all times part of our consciousness. And yet when speaking to each other or, indeed, when formulating our thoughts as writers, we tend to disregard these nonverbal elements of consciousness, although they may well have played an important part in evoking or at least coloring our thought. We tend, on the whole, to equate our consciousness merely with its verbal component, the stream of language that passes through our minds as an unending internal monologue. It might be thought that we are completely justified in doing so. Aren't these nonverbal elements of consciousness trivial in the extreme?

To a poet, Artaud would argue, it is precisely that nonverbal element of consciousness which is of supreme importance. For it is closely bound up with the very stuff and matter of poetry: human emotion.

What is emotion? It may be evoked by words, but it is not itself verbal. We are conscious of it, it often overwhelms our consciousness, but emotion certainly belongs to the nonverbal aspect of consciousness. And if we analyze the nature of emotion, we find that it is, however sublimated, however intensified, part and parcel of those very body sensations; that it differs only in degree from such lowly feelings as an overful stomach or, indeed, Artaud's nagging headaches. For whatever may have set off our emotions, we experience them as body sensations—a quickening of the pulse, a melting relaxation of muscular tensions, a rise in blood pressure, or the release of sex hormones with their various physiological effects. Fear and joy, the sublime beauty of a sunset, the arrival of the beloved, exaltation at hearing a beautiful poem, all are ultimately experienced as body sensations.

That is why the three words "I am cold" seemed to Artaud incapable of conveying what he actually experienced when he felt cold. To communicate emotion, which is the stuff of poetry, abstract words were not enough. That is why poetry makes use of concrete aspects of language which directly communicate to the body, elements such as the musical quality of the words, the sensual nature of the sounds they are made of, the rhythmic quality of the poem which directly activates the body's own rhythms—the beat of the blood—and the vast multitude of nonverbal associations inherent in language and activated by words.

The formula "I am cold," which abstracts all the body sensation, all the actual and complex feelings connected with one individual's experience of such a physical state, exemplified for Artaud the manner in which too glib a use of language desiccates experience and eventually makes people who rely on such modes of communication and thought lose contact with life itself. They seemed to him to substitute the mathematical formula, the abstract blueprint of experience for the complex fullness of the surging flood of existence in all its richness and complexity.

"The theater is the only place in the world and the last general means left to us to reach the organism directly and, in the period of neurosis and low sensuality into which we are about to plunge, to attack that low sensuality by physical means which it will not resist" (*OC* IV, 97). This is how Artaud put his realization, at which he had arrived by the mid-1930s, that the poetry he wanted to deal in transcended the merely verbal; and that the human body was both the instrument to be used in conveying his kind of poetry and the recipient of that poetry, to be exposed to it so as properly to experience its impact.

Artaud's ideas about a new technique and practice of theater (to be discussed in greater detail in the next chapter) are thus basically an attempt to communicate the fullness of human experience and emotion, bypassing the discursive use of language and establishing contact between the artist and his audience at a level above—or perhaps below—the merely cerebral appeal of the verbal plane. As at that stage he felt, or perhaps indeed *was*, incapable of bringing to bear the infinite variety of powerful and subtle techniques by which poetry *can* in fact be made capable of having so profound an impact that the fullness of human emotion, spiritual as well as physical, is communicated, he was burning to find ways and means of transmitting his experience, his physical suffering, his physical exaltation directly to the minds and bodies of other human beings. And to achieve that, he felt, he had to "smash language in order to touch life" (*OC* IV, 18).

This is how we have to understand his use of the term "theater of cruelty": He wanted the theater to swoop down upon a crowd of spectators with all the awesome horror of the plague, the Black Death of the Middle Ages, with all its shattering impact, creating a complete upheaval, physical, mental, and moral, among the populations it struck. "The theater, like the plague," he proclaims in perhaps the most powerfully poetic of the essays in *The Theater and Its Double*, "Le Théâtre et al peste,"

is a crisis which is resolved either in death or in the return to complete health. The plague is a superior evil because it is a total crisis after which nothing is left except death or utter purification. So also the theater is an evil because it is the supreme state of balance which cannot be reached without destruction. It asks the spirit to partake in a delirium which vastly enhances its energies. (*OC* IV, 38-39)

Statements like these display the fanatical fury with which Artaud pursued his objective, a commitment of truly mad heroism. The new language of the theater, a superior instrument of communication beyond the mere discursive use of concepts, language, and words, would establish a link through which the totality of emotion could freely flow from body to body, from actor to spectator. And this breaking down of the barriers between human beings, enabling them to partake in each others' most shattering emotions, would achieve no less than a new communion of mankind, a total transformation of society, and give to all human existence a greater richness and higher quality.

It is a grandiose vision, powered—one can feel this in

the prophetic sweep of the essays in *The Theater and Its Double*—by the rage and fury of frustration accumulated through his desperate efforts to bridge the gap between his feeling and its verbal expression. It is as though Artaud wanted to unleash the pent-up energies of this frustration in a vast liberating outburst of violence, of aggression against an unfeeling outside world, visualized as a mass of complacent, apathetic spectators in the theater who would find themselves engulfed, overwhelmed, and compelled to feel, to suffer as deeply as he himself, Antonin Artaud, had suffered.

If language alone had proved incapable of communicating the actual physical sensation of his painful struggles to other people, perhaps an assault upon their senses in the theater might wake them from their indifference and, by plunging them into equivalent pain and anguish, open their minds, shake them out of their apathy, and thus purify them morally. Artaud himself, always extremely lucid about his mental state, was fully aware of this rage, the pent-up aggression behind all his efforts. "Do you know another man," he asked Breton in 1937, shortly before his departure for Ireland, "whose indignation against everything which exists at present is as steady and violent; and who is so constantly and violently in a state of perpetual fulmination? This rage which consumes me, and of which every day I learn to make better use, must have some meaning" (*OC* IV, 38-39).

Even more than against the complacent bourgeois who neither knew nor cared for his suffering, this rage was directed against the system of thought, the whole cultural climate which had produced that attitude. Was not the complacency of these people built on the ideal of reason, moderation, *bienséance* which had animated French society for so long? And was not that ideal, in turn, the outcome of a belief in logic and thus ultimately in the correct use of language and reason as instruments of self-control? It was through an excessive reliance on the ability of logical discourse to find a just—and always moderate—solution to all problems that the springs of true feeling had been drained. Having left France for a country he believed nearer to these sources and still nourished by uncorrupted emotion, Mexico, Artaud warned his Mexican friends against the rationalism of Europe and the temptation to Mexicans to find themselves the heirs of "the Latin spirit, rational culture, the supremacy of reason" (OC VIII, 266). They still had, so Artaud believed, access to a richer experience through ritual, magic, and surrender to the wild transports of peyotl.

And yet the hopes that Artaud had pinned on the theater and his own ability to create a new language of physically embodied poetry came to nought. It is a tragic irony that it was through this collapse of his expectations and the breakdown it caused that he eventually bridged the chasm that had yawned between his emotion and its transmutation into words, and that he found his very own poetic language, a mode of utterance so powerful and direct that it was indeed capable of fully conveying the poet's emotion right down to the physical level of body sensations.

In writing to Soulié de Morant Artaud had wondered whether it was the intervention of the *will*, the conscious desire and determination to express himself, which made the thought and the emotion wanting to be expressed evaporate. In the mental turmoil which followed the catastrophe of *Les Cenci* and the deep disappointment after his return from Mexico Artaud reached such a pitch of nervous excitement that this last barrier of self-consciousness finally gave way. The *will*, the element of critical self-awareness which, in searching for the best possible turn of phrase, the most elegant image, had blocked the free flow between emotion and utterance, was swept aside in the wild exaltation of an artist who had, he felt, become an instrument of higher powers, a magician, a miracle-working prophet. The breathless frenzy with which he proclaimed his mission to save the world from impending doom imbues a text like that of *Les Nouvelles Révélations de l'Etre*, never intended to be poetry, with a sweep and intensity of vision which transmutes its language into that of a sublime poem, a poem, moreover, which, in its power to stir the imagination and the senses, is far superior to anything Artaud ever was able to achieve in the theater.

This inspired breakthrough into poetry was followed by years of stunned, catatonic silence in the asylums of Sotteville-lès-Rouen, Ste. Anne, and Ville Evrard. But after Artaud's arrival at Rodez, and even more so in the last frantic twenty months after his return to Paris, that seething, flaming lava stream of language flowed again. Writing feverishly by day and by night, Artaud produced an unceasing output in the form of essays, letters, personal confessions, rhythmic prose, glossolalia, and inarticulated combinations of consonants. It is difficult to decide which of these writings should be classified as poems, for all are deeply poetic, simply because they are direct and unalloyed expressions of profound emotion and triumphantly succeed in communicating that emotion through language.

It is another strange irony that in this phase of his career, many years after being expelled from the surrealist movement, Artaud should have realized the original aims of that movement more truly and totally than any of the poets the surrealists had themselves produced, for not even the greatest among these, whether Eluard, Desnos, or Aragon, had ever fully renounced the use of their technique, the intervention of their shaping critical intelligence in putting their poems on paper. Artaud in his prophetic fury—or madness, as it seemed to many—really allowed his wounded spirit to flow freely and without restraint; he fully attained the surrealists' objective, a technique of automatic writing which would give access to the darkest, deepest layers of the human mind and capture its movement at the very moment it emerged from the chasms and abysses of the unconscious into the light, of consciousness as poetry. Artaud himself, twenty-five years earlier, had been the director of the research center set up by the surrealists to investigate ways and means by which this objective could be achieved. Now he had become a living example of its attainment; but he had found the solution not, as he had then thought, by producing a neatly argued paper in smooth theoretical terms, but by having become himself the incarnation of that solution: that this type of poetry could be achieved only through a terrifying descent—or perhaps ascent—to hitherto unplumbed regions of human suffering and total self-abandonment. Putting aside all restraint, all intention of pleasing, of giving shape or formal perfection to his utterance, and letting his wild fantasies, his fury and anguish, his pain and torment roar out, Artaud succeeded in evoking that very physical impact, that gut-reaction which had been the objective of his theatrical endeavors. He wanted to make his last public appearance, the abortive radio program *Pour en finir avec le jugement de Dieu,* the true fulfillment of his ideas about the theater of cruelty; yet this sequence of texts was simply orchestrated for four voices and some percussion instruments. The performance, in particular Artaud's own spine-chilling screams and banging of gongs, added something to its effect, but its true "cruelty" (in the Artaudian sense of physical evocation of emotion) resides very largely in the words themselves, whether regarded as polemical pamphlets, autobiographical meditations, or "poems." Such is the degree of obsessiveness, of Artaud's possession by the passions which convulse him, that these texts appear as madly inspired as the utterances of the Pythia at Delphi talking in a holy trance, or the chants of a shaman through whom the voices of gods and demons speak.

It is difficult to analyze the means by which Artaud's writings at this period have their effect. *What* they say

(the discursive or conceptual element) is so wildly outside the customary bounds of reason that it contributes
as much to their physical effect (through the sheer
amazement or terror such descriptions inspire) as the
way they say it, the furious discordance and variation of
the rhythms, the abrupt transitions, the intensity evoked
by repetition and accumulation of words, all combining
to communicate the rage, anguish, and deep commitment which underlie them. Here language truly reaches
its utmost limit.

The Artaudian Theater—
Theory and Practice

iV

The theater
is the state
the place
the point
where we can get hold of man's anatomy and
through it heal and dominate life.

ARTAUD, from *Aliéner l'Acteur*, 12 May 1947

Artaud's ideas about the theater changed and
developed a great deal throughout his life. But
from the very beginning of his active involvement with the theater he was a fanatical believer in its mission, its power to change society,
man, and the world, its revolutionary potential
and redemptive force. He despised the view
that the theater was merely a place of entertainment. "There are those who go to the
theater as they go to the brothel," he started
an article for a Marseilles paper while working
with Dullin.

One might say that at this moment there are two different types of theater: a spurious theater, facile and false, the theater frequented by bourgeois, military men, rentiers, shopkeepers, winemerchants, teachers of watercolor painting, adventurers, whores, and winners of the Prix de Rome, which takes place at Sacha Guitry's, on the Boulevards, and in the Comédie Française; and another theater which finds a roof over its head where it can, but which is a theater conceived as the achievement of mankind's purest aspirations. (*OC* II, 175)

In this attitude he belonged to the mainstream of the movement for a renovation of the theater which had started as a reaction to its mid-nineteenth-century degradation into cheap melodrama and vulgar entertainment and was led by men like Ibsen, Strindberg, and Shaw, the Duke of Meiningen, Nietzsche, Richard Wagner, Adolphe Appia, Gordon Craig, Max Reinhardt, and Stanislavsky, and in France Antoine, Lugné Poe, Copeau, and Gémier. Dullin, Pitoeff, and Jouvet, with whom Artaud was in one way or another connected in his professional career, were the immediate heirs of this tradition, just as Jean-Louis Barrault and Roger Blin, who worked with Artaud in their beginnings, can be seen as its champions who continued it to our own day. Yet, while Artaud clearly forms part of this theatrical mainstream, he was also deeply at odds with it. For all its earnestness and reforming zeal, this movement for a return to theater as a serious art form had always remained within the framework of society; its standard-bearers and practitioners had worked within the usual professional and financial possibilities. Artaud's belief in the redemptive power of the theater, on the other hand, was so radical and uncompromising that he was in perpetual conflict with the established forms of theatrical enterprise. Yet to earn a living, and to gain a chance of working at all, he had somehow to come to terms with the world of theater owners, impresarios, influential patrons, and potential financial backers, and the tensions these attempts created within him proved well-nigh unbearable. In trying to understand Artaud's writings on the theater, therefore, one must always remember that his mind was frequently working at two distinct levels: In drawing up manifestos for his various projects he was at one and the same time enunciating his sweeping revolutionary ideas and trying to reassure the influential people he needed to support him. Thus, in the "First Manifesto for a Theater of Cruelty" in October 1932, which proclaimed his determination to diminish the importance of the playwright as against the director, he included the project of a production of Buechner's *Woyzeck*, "in a spirit of reaction against our principles and as an example of what one can achieve on the stage with a precise text" (*OC* IV, 119). By far the most glaring and disastrous example of the tension between Artaud's theoretical ideas and his need to try to find a *modus vivendi* with the theater as it was at that time is the production of *Les Cenci*, in which he had to cast an inexperienced actress because she gave him access to funds, use a theater building totally at variance with his ideas, and, in the final analysis, produce a play which, although he had written it himself, was far removed from his ideal of a theater beyond a conventional text and the traditional structure of classical tragedy, based on the movement of large numbers of performers in an open space.

It might be argued that, had his ideas been less extreme, he might have found it easier to gain a foothold in the theatrical establishment; or conversely that, had he found a foothold in the theatrical establishment sooner, say as a result of his work with the Théâtre Alfred Jarry, his ideas might never have become so extreme. But it is difficult to believe that the latter could ever have been the case. The programatic statements for the Théâtre Alfred Jarry contain the essence of Artaud's most radical concepts; the very first announcement of that enterprise makes the demand that the theater should never be mere play: "If the theater is not just play, if it is a true reality, by what means can we give it that degree of reality, make each performance a kind of event [*une sorte d'évènement* could also be translated as 'a kind of *happening*'—surely the first use of that term in this context!]? That is the problem we have to solve" (*OC* II, 19). This first manifesto describes a police raid on a brothel as the ideal theatrical event (or happening) and insists that each member of the audience, on leaving the theater,

> should have been shaken and taken aback by the internal power of the performance and that that power should be in direct relation to the anxieties and preoccupations of his life. The illusion will no longer be dependent on the probability or improbability of the action, but on the power to communicate and the reality of that action. . . . It is not to the mind or the senses of our audience that we address ourselves but to their whole existence. Theirs and ours. (*OC* II, 21)

The concept of the Theater of Cruelty is already present in these fighting words. And at about the same time Artaud (as the spokesman of his associates in the venture of the Théâtre Alfred Jarry) leaves no doubt about the sweep of his, and their, ambitions:

> We are aiming at no less than to go back to the human or inhuman sources of the theater and to revive it totally. Everything which forms part of the opacity and magnetic fascination of dreams, all this, these dark layers of consciousness . . . we want to see it triumph on the stage, at the risk of losing ourselves and exposing ourselves to the ridicule of a terrible failure. . . . We see the theater as a *truly magical* enterprise. We address ourselves not to the eyes, nor to the direct emotion of the mind; what we are trying to create is a certain *psychological* emotion in which

the most secret recesses of the heart will be brought into the open. (*OC* ii, 30-31)

Here are the guiding ideas of *The Theater and Its Double*, if not fully formed and elaborated, at least clearly recognizable: the theater as reality; the demand for an impact on the audience which amounts to an imposition of suffering on them, i.e. cruelty; the demand that the theater be able to communicate deep, subconscious, and therefore not yet verbalized emotion directly to the spectator by means that amount to nothing less than magic. Yet not until after the overwhelming experience of encountering the Balinese dancers in 1931 did Artaud's attitude to theater finally crystalize and acquire its explosive power, which can still be felt today. What was it that gave *The Theater and Its Double* that force?

In his book *Antonin Artaud et l'essence du théâtre*, Henri Gouhier questions Artaud's frequent demand that the theater return to its origins in religious ritual; he points out that while there is much great art which is religious, much very bad art, like those sugary statues in Catholic churches, is able to invoke genuine religious feeling; and there is also much very great art which is utterly nonreligious. Art therefore, he argues, quite correctly, can be great art only if it fulfills *artistic* criteria which are independent of religious considerations; and, indeed, if the theater's origins are in religious ritual, it became an art form precisely at the moment when the theater separated from ritual and turned into an autonomous activity. All this is convincing enough, but it misses Artaud's point: For Artaud the theater was not just a religious art, an art form serving a religion, but a manifestation of the religious impulse itself. His religion was the theater—at least up to the point when his profoundly religious nature led him into other even more intense and impassioned manifestations of his yearning to transcend the world as he had found it.

Yet how can the theater, a technique of communication which is generally regarded as capable of expressing a multitude of contents and messages and is therefore necessarily neutral, free of any philosophy or ideology, be turned into a religion? What kind of religion could the theater be?

For Artaud the theater was "activated metaphysics" (*OC* IV, 54). "The reservoir of energies constituted by Myths no longer incarnated by mankind, the theater incarnates them" (*OC* v, 272). The theater is the double (that is to say, the representative) "of that great magic active force [*agent*] of which the theater through its form is the figuration until the time when it becomes its transfiguration" (*OC* v, 272-73). And what are these great magic powers with which the theater can reestablish connection? They are "the secret truths" which the theater can again bring to light through its language of gesture, "that part of the truth buried under the forms in their encounter with the flow of Becoming" (*OC* v, 84). For all its seeming vagueness, the message is clear enough: Like Bergson, Shaw, or Nietzsche, Artaud was a romantic vitalist, a believer in the healing power of the life force, the power of man's natural instinct as against dry-as-dust rationalism and logical reasoning based on linguistic subtlety; he supported the heart against the head, the body and its emotions against the rarefied abstractions of the mind. But while Nietzsche in *The Birth of Tragedy* had proclaimed his conviction that the basis of the theater is the spirit of Dionysos, dark, violent, turbulent, passionate, inarticulate in its musical ecstasy, but tempered and tamed by Apollonian clarity, measure, and reason, Artaud rejected the Apollonian element altogether and put his trust in the dark forces of Dionysian vitality with all their violence and mystery. If these forces could be activated through the theater, incarnated by the theater, Artaud hoped that mankind might be diverted from the disastrous path that led toward increasing atrophy of the instincts, which amounted to the death of vitality and to eventual extinction.

Artaud's position also has parallels with Freud's view that the malaise of Western civilization was due to the repression of so much of man's instinctive, subconscious, impulsive life. A great deal of surrealist ideology was based on Freudian concepts, and Artaud was clearly influenced by Freud, in particular by the *Interpretation of Dreams*. Freud had indicated how language in dream is transposed into images which can then be read like picture-writing, hieroglyphs. Hence Artaud, in his endeavor to reactivate the subconscious and to appeal to it directly, preached a return to communication at this level. "It is not a question of suppressing articulate speech, but of giving it something of the importance it has in dreams" (*OC* IV, 112). But, above all, if the Dionysiac stands for instinct and the body and the Apollonian for the abstraction of bloodless reason and the mind, the theater is the means through which the body can again be given its due importance. Artaud's idea of a metaphysical theater, paradoxically, springs from his conviction that abstract, discursive thinking cuts man off from the hidden, mysterious sources of his being and confines him in a narrow mundane world. To reestablish contact with the true metaphysical basis of human existence the body must be reawakened and reactivated: In other words, to reach the metaphysical sphere we have to become more physical. Artaud's discovery of the Balinese dancers was a decisive event in his life because, through their strange movements and hieratic costumes, the miraculous music that accompanied their dance, the presence of cosmic power in their inarticulate cries, they were a revelation of the mysterious forces which rule the universe and made him realize the true nature of the theater as a potential instrument for the redemption of mankind. "I am not one of those who believe that civilization should change so that the theater can change; but I believe that the theater, used in a higher and the most difficult possible sense, has the power to influence the nature and development of things" (*OC* IV, 95).

In the theater, in Artaud's view, the cosmic forces, made manifest through physical means, can reach and touch the submerged physical, nonverbal, and subconscious energies of the masses. Hence his concept of a theater of cruelty.

But "theater of cruelty" means, above all, a theater difficult and cruel for myself. And on the level of performance it is not a matter of the cruelty we bring to bear upon each other in mutually cutting up our bodies, sawing at our personal anatomies or, like Assyrian emperors,[1] sending ourselves through the post bags of human ears, noses, or nostrils nicely cut up, but of that much more terrible and necessary cruelty which things can exercise upon ourselves. We are not free. The heavens can still fall upon our heads. And the theater exists, in the first place, to teach us that. (*OC* iv, 95)

Even though sublimated into forms subtler than direct physical assault, the Artaudian theater still relies on physical or near-physical action:

If music has an effect on snakes, this is not due to the spiritual concepts that it transmits to them, but because snakes are elongated and lie in long coils on the ground, which their bodies touch over almost their total length; and the musical vibrations which are propagated in the soil reach them as a very long and subtle massage; well, I intend to do to the audience what snake-charmers do and to make them reach even the subtlest notions through their organism. (*OC* iv, 97-98)

Artaud regarded the theater's ability (as he postulated it) to act physically upon a crowd of spectators without actually hurting their bodies as its chief distinguishing mark and, curiously, one that it shared with the plague.

[1] This is the passage which gave Arrabal the idea for his play, *The Architect and the Emperor of Assyria*.

In his essay "The Theater and the Plague" he dwells at length on the fact that, although filled with a black liquid, the body of the victim who has died of the plague shows no organic lesions. This, he argues, is comparable to

> the state of the actor whom his emotions totally overwhelm and shatter without an effect on reality. Everything in the physical aspect of the actor, as in that of the plague victim, shows that life has reacted to a paroxysm, and yet nothing has happened. . . . Where the images of the plague in relation with a powerful state of physical disorganization are like the last explosions of a spiritual force that is exhausting itself, the poetic images of the theater are a spiritual force which starts its trajectory in the senses and can then transcend reality. Once launched into his fury the actor needs infinitely more virtue to stop himself from committing a crime than an assassin needs courage to commit his; and it is here that the action of an emotion in the theater, in its purity (*gratuité*, i.e. disinterestedness), appears as infinitely more realization in action. (*OC* IV, 30-31)

In other words, the emotions in their manifestation in body sensations are real and true in a physical sense both in the actor and ultimately in the audience, but the actions which these emotions would in the real world entail remain potential: "A real theatrical experience shakes the calm of the senses, liberates the compressed unconscious, and drives toward a kind of potential revolt, which, however, cannot realize its full value, unless it remains potential and imposes on the assembled crowd a difficult and heroic attitude" (*OC* IV, 34).

The theater, as seen by Artaud in *The Theater and Its Double*, is essentially a religious ritual whose content, whose underlying myth, is the theater itself, that is, the theater defined as an assembly of human beings striving to establish contact with the profound mainsprings of their own being, the dark forces of physical emotion which lie beyond the trivialities of their everyday existence. The theater enables them to experience the full reality of these emotions without involving them in irreversible real-life situations in which alone experiences of such shattering power could otherwise be lived through. And by making the full force of a full emotional life, the whole gamut of human suffering and joy, again active in multitudes of human beings, the theater could change their basic attitude to life and institutions, their ways of thinking, their entire consciousness, and thus transform society and the world.

But *how*, by what means and methods, is all this to be accomplished?

Above all, the playwright disappears as the main fountainhead of the theatrical experience. This, for Artaud, was the principal and overwhelming lesson of the Balinese theater: "The Balinese realize, with the utmost rigor, the idea of a pure theater, in which everything, conception as well as execution, is valid and exists only in the measure in which it is objectivized *on the stage*. They victoriously demonstrate the absolute preponderance of the director whose creative power *eliminates the words* (*OC* IV, 64-65). Artaud's theater is essentially a director's theater with the director as a poet using the concrete language of the whole gamut of physical existence from abstract space to the minutest nuance of the actor's bodily movement.

This stage language will not dispense with words but will use them as they appear in dreams, and will draw the fullest possible effect from the quality of words as objects with a physical existence, as sounds in cries, sobs, incantation, and an infinite variety of expressive colors. A technique will have to be found for recording and transcribing the multitude of modes of expression of the nonverbal language of the stage, for each gesture, each movement, each intonation will have a definite and precise expressive meaning comparable to that of

Chinese ideograms or Egyptian hieroglyphics. Yet, unlike those systems of signs, which have to be laboriously learned, the new stage language of concrete signs will have the power of immediately communicating the exact meaning of each hieroglyphic sign or symbol to the audience. This communicative power, which springs from the direct physical effect achieved by what happens on the stage, constitutes the true magic of the theater.

The largest theatrical element with a direct and immediate physical effect is the space in which the theatrical event occurs. The traditional theater building will be abandoned. In the Artaudian theater there will be no barrier between actors and audience. "The spectator placed in the middle of the action is enveloped and covered by it" (*OC* IV, 115). At first hangars or barns can be used for this purpose; later special buildings will be constructed on the pattern of certain churches or "certain temples in the highlands of Tibet" (*OC* IV, 115). The audience will be seated in the middle of these spaces on seats which will be moveable so that they can follow the action developing around them on all sides. The walls of the auditorium will be whitewashed in light-absorbing chalk. An elevated gallery running around the auditorium will enable the action to take place at several levels. There will be no scenery. The splendor of the costumes will be sufficient to give the action vividness and color, particularly as each costume will convey its own precise hieroglyphic meaning. Modern dress, with it drabness and suggestion of the naturalistic and psychologizing conventional theater, should be avoided. On the other hand, wholly new and revolutionary lighting equipment will have to be designed to produce magical effects of great meaning; these will include vibrating light, waves of light, or veritable explosions of light resembling fireworks. The light will have to have a wide variety of color and tonal qualities, such as tenseness, density, and opacity, to produce the impression of warmth, cold, fury, or fear. Music and sound will also have to play a very important part; ancient and forgotten instruments may have to be used or completely new ones invented, some of which will have to be able to produce "sounds which cannot be endured" (*OC* IV, 114). And of course natural sounds, which Artaud used with stereophonic effect in his production of *Les Cenci,* also enter into the arsenal of auditory effects. Artaud attached special importance also to large puppets, which would appear in the action and produce magical effects of dreamlike fantasy or surprise. In the "First Manifesto for a Theater of Cruelty" he makes an enigmatic reference to "puppets thirty feet high, representing King Lear's beard in the storm" (*OC* IV, 117).

Although always ritual and magic, the Artaudian theater is by no means to be without humor. Indeed the element of humor, which Artaud conceived of as a dislocation of sensibility through anarchy, the juxtaposition of incompatible elements which turns the expected order of things upside down, is to play an important part in the peculiar poetic ambiance of his theatrical creations. He quotes, as an example, a scene from a Marx Brothers film (he loved the Marx Brothers and included a note on them in *The Theater and Its Double*) in which a man who thinks he is about to kiss a beautiful lady suddenly finds that he is holding a cow in his arms. Artaud was fully aware that his conception of a theater-in-the-round with full audience involvement approached old traditions of spectacle hitherto on the margin of theater, like the circus and the music hall, burlesque, and vaudeville. He wanted to draw every possible lesson from these.

What then, finally, in this director's theater, about the actor? His role, said Artaud in a letter to Gaston Gallimard at the time he was planning to launch a theater with the support of the *NRF,* is "at the same time extremely important and extremely limited. What one calls the personality of the actor must disappear completely. There can no longer be an actor who imposes his rhythm on the *ensemble* and to whose personality everything must be subordinated. . . . In the theater the actor as such must no longer have the right to any initiative whatever" (*OC* v, 125). On the other hand, as a theater based on a complex language of fixed signs, gestures and expressions will require very great skill, the Artaudian theater will need "strong" actors "who will be chosen not because of their talent but on the strength of a kind of vital sincerity, which is stronger than their convictions" (*OC* v, 126). In the prospectus of the Théâtre Alfred Jarry Artaud had promised that the performances directed by him "would proceed in the manner of a perforated music roll in a mechanical piano . . . and would give to the auditorium the impression of fatality and the most precise predetermination" (*OC* ii, 612).[2]

On the other hand Artaud devoted much thought to the techniques of acting. One of the most remarkable of the essays in *The Theater and Its Double,* which, though least often quoted and understood, has had the most far-reaching influence in that it helped Jean-Louis Bar-

---

[2] Artaud's insistence on this high degree of prerehearsed and predetermined precision—the very antithesis of improvization—seems, as Jacques Derrida has pointed out in a famous essay, "Le Théâtre de la Cruauté et la clôture de la représentation" (included in the volume *L'Ecriture et la différence*), to be in contradiction with two passages in *The Theater and Its Double* (*OC* iv, 91, 99) in which Artaud seems to insist on the uniqueness and unrepeatability of each theatrical event. Derrida links these passages with quotations from Artaud's much later writings in which he denied the possibility of theater altogether. On closer inspection, however, the passages from *The Theater and Its Double* quoted by Derrida are taken out of context and refer to quite different points: the first passage to the unrepeatability of fixed statements such as are contained in recognized classical, but now dead, works; and the second to the irreversibilty of actions in *reality,* which the theater, however, by sublimating the emotion, *can* make repeatable.

rault to develop his theory of acting, is "Un Athlétisme affectif" (which might be rendered as "The Actor, an Athlete of his Emotions"). In it, Artaud lays the foundation (on the basis of the teaching of the Cabbala) for a complete and complex system of breathing and expressive techniques in which each type of breath corresponds to a basic emotional color, which can be infinitely varied by permutation and combination. Artaud's language is obscure and it is, above all, difficult to visualize what he means without direct demonstration by a teacher. But the basis is a number of triads based on, for example, (1) breathing in, (2) breathing out, and (3) retaining the breath. Linking one's mode of utterance to each of these three possibilities produces distinct expressive colors; so does another triad, such as placing the voice (1) in the diaphragm, (2) in the chest, or (3) in the head. Taking these six expressive possibilities as the primary colors, one can then vary and permutate them by placing the voice in the head while breathing out, or in, or retaining the breath, and so on. Artaud uses concepts like masculine, feminine, and neuter and makes reference to *yin* and *yang* and the 380 points of Chinese acupuncture. If one knows how to translate this technical and mystical language into mundane physical practice the results, as anyone who has watched Barrault demonstrate this technique (or rather his élaboration of it) can testify, are spectacular. As Artaud says in his essay, it is through breathing and other physical links that the identification between the actor's and the spectator's body is established. This is the chain which links them together and "allows the spectator to identify himself with the performance breath by breath, and bar by bar. . . . All emotion has organic bases. It is in cultivating his emotion in his body that the actor recharges the density of its voltage. Knowing in advance which parts of the body one wants to touch means putting the spectator into magic trances" (*OC* IV, 163).

So much for the actor in the Artaudian theater. And

who should form its public? In the "First Manifesto of the Theater of Cruelty" Artaud deals with the matter thus: "The Public: First the theater must exist" (*OC* IV, 118).

This, in brief outline, is Artaud's view of a new theater, as described in the essays collected in *The Theater and Its Double*, written between 1931 and 1936. The "First Manifesto of the Theater of Cruelty" contained an impressive list of projected performances: an adaptation of an Elizabethan play, perhaps *Arden of Faversham*, which André Gide was translating; a poetic drama by Léon-Paul Fargue; an adaptation of a story from the *Zohar*, by Rabbi Siméon; the story of Blue-Beard, as reconstructed from the archives; the Fall of Jerusalem, according to the Bible and history; an adaptation of a story by the Marquis de Sade; one or several romantic melodramas the very improbability of which would become a poetic element; Buechner's *Woyzeck*; and some works of the Elizabethan theater, stripped of their text so that only characters, plot, and period flavor remain. In the "Second Manifesto of the Theater of Cruelty," issued as a prospectus in 1933, only one performance is projected, Artaud's own *La Conquête du Mexique*, which existed as a scenario, a blueprint for a production to be created in rehearsal. When some of these plans finally materialized in 1935 with *Les Cenci*, relatively little of Artaud's theoretical concept could be translated into practice. There was the music emanating from loudspeakers in the four corners of the auditorium and there was Artaud's own frantic acting, but the sets and costumes, though excellent, were conventional, and so was the play.

To judge by the consensus of opinion of those who saw Artaud act in the theater, he was an uneven and probably rather bad actor. Barrault is on record that he

took drugs which tranquilized him or pepped him up or gave him the illusion that he had found a certain equilibrium; he was rather like a man in a dream who thinks he has solved a problem while dreaming and then, when he wakes up the next morning, his problem has remained unsolved. There were certainly sublime moments in his acting, but they were suddenly contradicted by dissonances over which he had no control.[3]

As a director, in the case of *Les Cenci*, he had difficulty in explaining to the actors what he wanted them to do. Blin has described how, in arranging the banquet scene in *Les Cenci*, Artaud told the actors who were playing the guests to assume, each of them, the movements of a different animal; the actors simply did not know how to put that suggestion into practice. Whether with sufficient means and time at his disposal Artaud could ever have succeeded in putting his own ideas into practice must remain an open question.

During his period of confinement Artaud only occasionally revived his interest in the theater. His religious instinct had found other, even more passionately committed outlets. But after his return from Rodez he again talked about the theater and wrote poems about it. But in most of these the term "theater" appears in a different sense: It seems almost as though "theater" and "life" had become interchangeable:

> The true theater has always seemed to me the exercise of a terrible and dangerous act
> in which, moreover, the idea of theater and performance is eliminated just as
> that of all science, all religion, and all art . . .[4]

Or even:

> And now I want to say something which might perhaps astonish many people.
> I am the enemy

---

[3] Jean-Louis Barrault, quoted in Jean-Louis Brau, p. 97.
[4] *"Le Théâtre et la Science"* (1947).

of the theater.
I have always been that.
As much as I love the theater,
As much am I, for that very reason, its enemy . . .[5]

In many of these deeply moving poems the specter of the theater seems to float across Artaud's consciousness, with many of the metaphysical ideas and much of the religious fervor of his belief in its redemptive mission still shining through, almost like memories only half recalled:

The plague,
cholera,
the black pocks only
exist because the dance
and consequently the theater
have not yet begun to exist . . .[6]

When the radio program *Pour en finir avec le jugement de Dieu* was in preparation it was said that Artaud regarded it as the first real public presentation of his ideas of a Theater of Cruelty, just as to some observers his courageous and heartrending exposure of his sufferings at the public lecture at the Vieux Colombier in January 1947 had seemed the ultimate merging of reality and its public exhibition as a performance—hence the true theater of cruelty. After the banning of the broadcast Artaud wrote to his friend Paule Thévenin, who had helped him so much in its creation, and announced, deeply disappointed, that he had for ever given up the idea of working through a mechanical medium:

Where the machine is
there is always an abyss and nothingness . . .

And he went on:

[5] December, 1946.
[6] *Le Théâtre de la Cruauté*, 19 November 1947.

And I shall henceforth devote myself
exclusively
to the theater
as I understand it
a theater of blood
a theater which at every performance will have
     achieved some gain

bodily
to him who plays as well as to him who comes to see
     the playing,
moreover
one doesn't play
one acts.
The theater is in reality the genesis *of creation.*
It will be done.

This poem in the form of a letter is dated 24 February 1948. Artaud died on 4 March.

It is impossible to read *The Theater and Its Double* or an account of its contents today without realizing how powerful and widespread its influence has proved to be. It took a long time for that influence to make itself felt, particularly in France. Barrault and Blin, the two major younger directors who had been under Artaud's most immediate influence in their formative years, both went their own ways. Barrault has said that he derived great benefit from Artaud's method of the expressive triads, but he also remained firmly wedded for many years to a theater based on accepted texts; he even became the chief proponent of Artaud's early *bête noire*, Claudel. Roger Blin, whose work served writers who had been close personal friends of Artaud, like Arthur Adamov, and also played a part in bringing to prominence such giants of the postwar avant-garde as Beckett and Genet, has pointed out that Artaud's influence on him was in the main indirect, in that it showed him a model of total dedication and uncompromising artistic purity but did not lead him to adopt any specifically Artaudian style or method.

Outside France Artaud's influence on the theater came into its own after the rise to fame and prominence of the postwar French avant-garde had drawn the attention of those interested in the art of drama to the tradition that stretches from Jarry, Apollinaire, and the surrealists to Beckett and Ionesco. The part Artaud had played in shaping that tradition was gradually recognized after a translation of *The Theater and Its Double* appeared in the United States in 1958.

Peter Brook and Charles Marowitz gave public recognition to the discovery of Artaud as one of the founders of modern avant-garde theater by calling their 1964 season of experimental acting and staging at the LAMDA theater (which was to prepare the Royal Shakespeare Company's ensemble for the difficult task of producing Jean Genet's *The Screens* under Peter Brook's direction, a project which never reached fruition in public) "Theater of Cruelty." This highly successful season, presenting what essentially amounted to training sessions or rehearsals in public, included what must have been the first performance of Artaud's sketch *Le Jet de sang* (*The Spurt of Blood*), a skit on a romantically lyrical piece by Salacrou, dating from 1925. While this early playlet did not demonstrate Artaud's ideas very clearly, other experiments inspired by his demand for expression without the use of articulate language but through a heightened expressiveness of the body proved highly interesting. The ten actors who had been trained by Brook and Marowitz during this experimental season—they included Glenda Jackson—became the nucleus of Brook's highly successful production of Peter Weiss's *Marat/Sade* by the RSC which again made use of Artaud's ideas, particularly in the treatment of madness in the portrayal of the majority of the characters, who are inmates of a lunatic asylum.

Peter Brook's further researches at his experimental workshop in Paris in later years also centered on Artaud's postulate of a theater transcending the limitations of language. Brook tried to evolve an expressive idiom based on gesture, movement, and incantatory sound which would be understood even without a knowledge of the meaning of the words. These efforts culminated in a spectacle, created for the Festival at Persepolis in 1971, for which Brook asked the poet Ted Hughes to invent a wholly new language, "Orghast," designed to be expressive through sound alone. Peter Brook's more conventional work, notably his widely acclaimed *Midsummer Night's Dream*, applied some of the lessons learned from these experiments with brilliant success: Here too Artaud's influence could be seen in the emphasis on physical expressiveness and acrobatic prowess in the acting, the techniques of the circus and music hall used in the staging, and the way in which magical effects were produced by a combination of subtle refinement and artless naivety, very much in the spirit of the Balinese and oriental folk-traditions so highly praised and recommended by Artaud.

Jerzy Grotowski, the brilliant Polish director, whose ideas and practice have much in common with Artaud, had no knowledge of Artaud's writings until after he achieved international fame and success. Nevertheless the similarity between Artaud and Grotowski is striking. This is probably due to the fact that Grotowski, who wanted to study theater outside his native Poland, was sent by the Polish authorities to China; hence he received inspiration from theatrical techniques very near to the oriental models Artaud admired. Grotowski, like Artaud, believes in the theater as a metaphysical force, only justified if it can truly transform the lives of both actors and spectators. He demands from his company, as did Artaud, a dedication which amounts to a veritable immersion in the theater as a holy rite and quasi-religious practice. Like Artaud he uses incantation and extracts maximum expressiveness from the human body. He insists on audiences of no more than about forty or fifty spectators, in order to expose them to the most direct physical impact from the actors. And like Artaud, he insists on the abandonment of the conventional theater architecture; he creates a new spatial concept for each of his productions.

The influence of Artaud's ideas is clearly discernible also in the work of three Latin American directors active in France: Jorge Lavelli, Jerome Savary, and Victor Garcia. Garcia, for example, used swiveling seats for a production of Arrabal's *Le Cimetière de voitures* in Paris some years ago and made the action take place all around the spectators, who at times were furiously rotating in their seats. Lavelli is a master of magical effects of sound and light. Savary's *Grand Magic Circus* combines elements of circus and ritual, fiction and reality, very much in the spirit of Artaud.

The American avant-garde theater also owes many impulses to Artaud, notably in the work of Judith Malina's and Julian Beck's Living Theater, Joseph Chaikin's Open Theater, and Richard Schechner's Performance Group. They too reject conventional theatrical space and rely on physical expressiveness as against the spoken word, the direct impact on the spectator of events which might be real *or* fictional, improvisation, audience involvement, etc. Whether Peter Schumann, in his work with giant puppets at the Bread and Butter Theater, is indebted to Artaud or to Central European folk festivals, his striking and beautiful supermarionettes certainly correspond to Artaud's ideas.

Among the younger generation in France, Ariane Mnoujkine's Théâtre du Soleil, with its conception of multifocussed spectacles in an unstructured space where the audience freely moves from one area of action to another, clearly owes an immense debt to Artaud, notably with *1789* and *1793* and *L'Age d'Or*. And after his expulsion from the Théâtre National de l'Odéon in

1968, Jean-Louis Barrault too showed himself willing to use some of the ideas of his old companion-in-arms, performing his spectacle based on Rabelais in a circus, and later converting the Gare d'Orsay into a space for theatrical performance.

In Italy Luca Ronconi brilliantly translated Artaudian concepts into theatrical reality with his *Orlando Furioso*, another spectacle staged in an unstructured space in which the ingenious use of moveable rostrums created a multitude of different stages and acting areas, with the audience freely milling around among giant puppets of horses and knights-in-arms jousting and battling, while weird fairytale monsters flew through the air and giant dragons were cut in half. Here Artaud's view that his kind of theater, far from being an esoteric game for aesthetes and intellectuals, should become a true folk spectacle like the circus and the music hall can be said to have found spectacular justification and confirmation. The same applies to Ronconi's daring and original adaptation of several plays by Aristophanes, *Utopia*, in which trucks and motor cars and even an airplane moving in procession through a space shaped like a road create a multifocal stage that makes the show pass before the audience like a Renaissance *trionfo*.

And, finally, Artaud's postulate that the theater should merge with real life to form a genuine *event* has no doubt inspired and influenced the movement toward a new form, the Happening. In spite of some spectacular successes this still seems to be in its early stages of development. But its potential and prospects seem far-reaching, provided that, as Artaud had always demanded, poets of genius can be found to put their imagination and creative power to its service.

That Artaud's theoretical writings have borne fruit is evident from this brief and selective account of some of the theatrical ventures that owe him a debt. Whether those or any others that might yet follow in their wake will in fact transform human sensibility and consciousness to such a degree that a new theater will lead to a transformed society and world is another question which only time can answer.

What is, however, clear even now is that outside the theater itself Artaud's concepts are strangely gaining in relevance. For example, Artaud's postulate that theater and life should merge, that a police raid on a brothel was in some sense the perfect balletlike theatrical happening, has been met, not in the theater, but in the documentary film and, above all, in radio and television, in which reality is used as the raw material for a dramatically structured presentation of life.

Artaud, who earned most of his living through acting in films, had a highly ambivalent attitude toward the cinema. He clearly saw its potential as an art form using images of the real world; his own film scenario of a surrealistic sequence of images, *La Coquille et le clergyman*, shows his understanding of the language of moving pictures. But his disappointment about the way in which Germaine Dulac had directed that film and his experiences with the commercial directors for whom he worked thoroughly disillusioned him and led him, eventually, to hate it. His experience with radio in the last months of his life proved equally disillusioning.

Nevertheless the electronic mass media and the cinema are, in fact, the fulfillment of at least part of Artaud's vision. Directors like Jean-Luc Godard and Michelangelo Antonioni produce profound metaphysical drama through the use of physical reality, immediate, spontaneous, and yet meticulously and deliberately shaped and structured. The seeming inner contradiction between Artaud's insistence on utter reality and spontaneity on the one hand, and the most precise and premeditated artistry on the other, *can* be overcome by the combination of a recording on film of immediate, spontaneous reality and its exact and deliberate structuring by editing. And the techniques of television, which can record events as they happen and transmit them at the same moment, while immediately structuring them by cutting from one camera to another, as in the televising of sports events, political and religious ritual (church services, coronations), military actions, or street demonstrations, are even more closely in conformity with some of Artaud's visionary theoretical pronouncements.

And, indeed, through these techniques Artaud's insistence that Theater is the double of Life and Life the double of Theater has increasingly been vindicated. More and more in our time, while the theater (or drama, of which the theater is only one special case) is increasingly striving to become more closely linked with life (as in the Happenings movement or theater-in-the-round), life is becoming increasingly theatricalized. The theater is becoming more and more political and politics more and more theatrical.

Artaud's visions, which seemed the fantasies of a visionary in the 1930s, can now be seen to have been truly prophetic.

More Devils Than Vast Hell Can Hold

V

And what is an authentic madman? It is a
man who has preferred to go mad, in the
sense in which society understands the term,
rather than be false to a certain superior
idea of human honor. That is why society has
had all those of whom it wanted to rid itself,
against whom it wanted to defend itself because they had refused to become its accom-
plices in certain acts of supreme filthiness,
condemned to be strangled in its asylums.
For a madman is also a man to whom society
did not want to listen and whom it wanted to
prevent from uttering unbearable truths.

ARTAUD, *OC* XIII, 17

That is how Artaud, in his impassioned defense
of van Gogh, which was also a strong plea for
his own cause, raised a question which to this
day, thirty years later, is a subject of heated and
urgent debate, the question as to the true nature
of madness and society's attitude to it; and above

all the controversy about the function of the psychiatrist. After nine years in a variety of asylums Artaud had strong views on that subject: "It is almost impossible to be a doctor and an honest man at the same time, but it is damned impossible to be a psychiatrist without at the same time being tarred by the brush of the most indisputable madness: that of being unable to fight that ancient, atavistic mob reflex which makes any scientist in the grip of the mob a born, a congenital enemy of all genius (*OC* XIII, 31). But while he proclaimed that it was medicine which had created disease and that psychiatrists were determined to exterminate all men of genius, he also, in the same strange piece of prose, half essay, half poem, returned to the conviction he had nursed through the years of his confinement: that the real cause of his suffering and that of other kindred spirits of genius had been occult, a vast conspiracy to put a spell on him and his like: "That is why unanimous spells were cast on Baudelaire, Edgar Poe, Gérard de Nerval, Nietzsche, Kierkegaard, Hölderlin, Coleridge, and also van Gogh. It can happen by day, but by preference it happens generally in the night." (*OC* XIII, 18).

And yet Artaud was conscious of the fact that notions like that of being bewitched or put under a spell were, in some sense, no more than poetic metaphors: "What, after all, is a poet," he wrote to one of the psychiatrists at Rodez in January 1945, "if not a man who visualizes and makes concrete his ideas and his images more intensely and with more telling appropriateness than other people, and gives them, through the rhythm of language, the character of fact" (*OC* XI, 11).

And if, at times, he became violent, was that not understandable in his situation? In defending van Gogh and trying to explain his suicide as the effect of the treatment he had received from society, Artaud made the point: "I have myself spent nine years in a lunatic asylum and have never suffered from the obsession of wanting to kill myself; but I know that each conversation with a psychiatrist, in the morning, made me want to hang myself because I knew I could not strangle him" (*OC* XIII, 38).

Yet from the very beginning of his career as a writer and man of the theater Artaud not only knew that he was suffering from a nervous or psychological ailment, that he was a *case* of outstanding interest, but prided himself on it. His dependence on, and attachment to, psychiatrists like Dr. Toulouse and Dr. Allendy show that he felt himself in need of help, if only to cure his persistent headaches and his difficulties in putting his thoughts on paper. The correspondence with Rivière, in which he meticulously describes these difficulties as amounting to a loss of personality, a loss of the sense of existing at all, indicates that his trouble lay deeper than mere migraine. His abortive attempt to have himself psychoanalyzed by Dr. Allendy also bears this out.

In fact, the knowledge that he was different from other people, that he was destined to suffer, became a vital part of his sense of identity. It was this aspect of his personality—the essay on van Gogh clearly shows this—which enabled him to regard himself as a member of that select band of Nerval, Poe, Nietzsche, Kierkegaard, Hölderlin, and Coleridge (though he finally rejected Coleridge and wrote an essay, "Coleridge the Traitor," in which he denounced him, who had once been a great poet and dreamer of opium dreams, for having killed his own soul to live the life of a bourgeois). And as he never saw himself as, never wanted to be, a run-of-the-mill, *normal* human being, as he was proud of his separateness, his claim to be exceptional, in fact a genius, the issue between Artaud and society never really amounted to a debate whether he was mad or not (if madness implied an exceptional psychological make-up, different and remote from drab normality) but merely whether society was entitled to incarcerate him for nine years under abominable conditions which for most of the time amounted to calculated brutality and torture. And if, during part of that period, he suffered from violent tantrums or extreme symptoms of withdrawal, was that not due to the shock he had suffered when he was suddenly clapped into a straitjacket and imprisoned? If, as was undoubtedly the case, this sudden arrest was due to his having caused a disturbance in the streets of Dublin, and then, on the *Washington,* having attacked the men who entered his cabin, the cause of Artaud's violent behavior was clearly no more than an unfortunate misunderstanding arising from his inability to grasp questions addressed to him in a foreign language. Apart from this, his behavior before his confinement, though odd, had never been a menace to society. He may have paraded through the Latin Quarter of Paris brandishing his miraculous cane and striking sparks from the pavement with its metal point while uttering loud prophetic curses, but that had never done anyone any harm.

Of course, the decisions to go to Mexico and, even more, to set out on the journey to Ireland while in a state of apocalyptic exaltation could hardly be described as outstandingly rational acts. Yet had not society, by its refusal to give him an opportunity to realize his artistic ideas without compromising his integrity, literally driven him out into the wilderness? But on the other hand, was not this rejection and the martyrdom of confinement as a lunatic, in a higher sense, the only way in which he could fully realize his destiny and establish the identity which made him the adored idol of posterity? These are questions which are truly unanswerable, as unanswerable as the question, *mutatis mutandis,* whether Pontius Pilate and Judas Iscariot should be blamed for having caused the Crucifixion or praised for having enabled the divine plan to be fulfilled.

Be that as it may, Artaud's preoccupation with his own predicament, his lucidity even in periods of extreme mental tension, and his genius as a writer have made his story one of the best documented case histories of all time, on a par with the writings of the Marquis de Sade or Daniel Paul Schreber. The brilliance with which he described his writing difficulties and the spontaneity of his utterances in his last years, which allow profound and immediate insights into the workings of the deepest recesses of the human psyche, probably make Artaud's *oeuvre* even more valuable than these classics of human self-revelation.

The first question which Artaud's case raises is that of the organic origin of his nervous disability. Whether or not the supposed attack of meningitis which he suffered at the age of five really was, as is often assumed, the source of all his troubles, he repeatedly mentioned that from the age of six he had undergone periods of stuttering, nervous contractions of the facial muscles and the tongue, and later

> spasms of pain in the right side of the neck which cut my breathing . . . limbs which become numb and begin to prickle, violent itching which suddenly moves from the arms to the legs, the spinal column full of crackles, painful on top. A violent weakness, ready to drop to the ground, which is an amplification of the unbearable compression of the head and the shoulder-blades. At times a general cramp which comes and goes, at others all the feelings of intense fever: cramp, heat, shivering, droning noises in the ears, pain caused by light. (*OC* 1 Suppl., 89-90)

In the letter to Dr. Allendy in which he gives this catalogue of ailments, dated 22 March 1929, Artaud makes a special point of assuring the doctor that all these symptoms had appeared although he had stopped taking drugs weeks ago. If these, however, *were* withdrawal symptoms, it must be remembered that he had started to take laudanum ten years earlier precisely because he had been advised that it would stop these physical discomforts. Or could all these symptoms have had a psychological origin?

In another long letter describing his disability to the acupuncturist Soulié de Morant, in February 1932, Artaud categorically stated that his physical symptoms had been "complicated by psychological troubles which only appeared *in a spectacular fashion* at the age of nineteen" (*OC* 1 Suppl., 130). This was the time when, as he told Jean Hort, he had destroyed all his youthful writings and given his books away to his friends. It was the onset of this depression which led to his first stay at a sanatorium. And it is also the exact moment when the incident of his being stabbed by a pimp, which he dwelt on a great deal in his period of confinement, is supposed to have happened.

What kind of psychological trauma could Artaud have suffered in his adolescence? "Until my twenty-seventh year," he said in a lecture in Mexico in 1936,

I lived with an obscure hatred of the Father, and of my own father in particular. To the day I saw him die. Then that inhuman severity with which I accused him of treating me suddenly ceased. Another being emerged from that body. And for the first time in my life my father stretched out his arms toward me. And I, who suffer from unease in my body, understood that he had suffered unease in his body, and that there is a lie in existence against which we are born to protest. (*OC* VIII, 178)

Another traumatic event in his early life to which he often referred was the death of his infant sister Germaine, aged seven months, when he was not yet nine years old. While it would be vain to speculate on the nature of possible feelings of guilt about this event, it is certainly striking that the subject which most attracted him in the theater was incest: In the early playlet, *Le Jet de sang*, there is a scene of incest between a young man and his sister, followed by a series of horribly disgusting erotic images of old women. Artaud's only detailed analysis of a play, which he introduced as an example of the Theater of Cruelty in *The Theater and Its Double*, is that of John Ford's *'Tis Pity She's a Whore*, also involving incest between brother and sister; and *Les Cenci* describes the incestuous rape of a daughter by her father, followed by the horrible murder of the guilty parent. In the years of his confinement when he was drawing up lists of the women he had most loved in his life, Artaud always called these his *daughters*, even though they usually included his two grandmothers, the sisters Neneka and Cathérine Schili.

The element of sexual guilt feelings also strongly emerges from his violent refusal to admit any suggestion that he might be suffering from the aftereffects of syphilis. Shortly after his arrival at Rodez he wrote to one of the doctors, pointing out that the fact that his pupils were unequal in size could not possibly imply that he might himself have contracted syphilis (which could only, in his case, be congenital), "because I do not know and despise all sexual relations of whatever kind as being degrading for man, and it is therefore a grave insult to me for anyone to believe that my body could ever have indulged in these at any moment in my life" (*OC* x, 13). He went on to complain bitterly that because the inequality of his pupils had been taken for an indication that he suffered from the aftereffects of syphilis, he had ever since 1917 been subjected to an endless succession of injections with substances ranging from mercury to novarsenobenzole which had greatly aggravated his nervous condition.

Artaud's total rejection of all sex from the period of the collapse of his theatrical hopes onward, which led to his elaboration of a complete mythology according to which God had created man without sexual and digestive organs, and man had been degraded into a sexual and defecating being by the intervention of evil extraterrestrial forces (a belief which he maintained even after he had again abandoned the fervent Christianity to which he had been converted before his transfer to

Rodez), also point to a regression to an early period of violent sexual guilt. In some of his writings toward the end of his life he went so far as to deny ever having owed his own life to a sexual act between his parents: "I, Antoine Artaud, I am my son, my father, my mother. (*OC* XII, 77).

> *Je ne crois à ni père*
> > *ni mère*
> *ja ne pas*
> *a papa-mama* (*OC* XII, 99)

The violent rage, "the fury which has been rising in me for forty-nine years" (*OC* IX, 193), as he called it when he was forty-nine years old, is another aspect of Artaud's personality which points to deep pent-up guilt feelings and frustrations translating themselves into aggressiveness. The concept of the Theater of Cruelty through which mankind was to be shaken out of its complacency and contentment and to be made aware of the depth of emotion and suffering beneath the calm surface of its life could well be regarded, in the last analysis, as a violent assault against humanity as a whole.

There is also a link between Artaud's aggressiveness against a world unaware of his mental and physical torments and the whole complex of drug addiction which eventually became one of the main inner motivations of his elaborate gnostic mythology. In a document dating from the beginnings of his association with the surrealists, which was published on 1 January 1925, Artaud made an impassioned plea for the free use of opium as the only possible remedy for a long list of sufferers, including "lucid madmen, tabetics, cancer patients, and those afflicted with chronic meningitis," whom he addressed, with obvious fellow feeling:

> You are outside life, you are above life, you are afflicted with ills the ordinary person does not know, you transcend the normal level and that is what

people hold against you, you poison their quietude, you corrode their stability. You feel repeated and fugitive pain, insoluble pain, pain outside thought, pain which is neither in the body nor the mind, but which partakes of both. And I, who share your ills, I am asking: Who should dare to restrict the means that bring us relief? (*OC* VIII, 25)

Artaud used to emphasize at this period of his life that he did not resort to opium and similar drugs because of the pleasures of intoxication, but simply as a relief from pain, as a medicine he needed to enable him to work. In a text which remained unpublished at the time but on which he was working in 1934 he stressed that it was "a state outside life [the loss of the sense of self from which he had suffered from puberty] which made me one day resort to opium. I have not been able to get rid of it and never shall" (*OC* VIII, 25). And, although he regarded opium as an "abominable swindle," he needed it, though "it is not opium which enables me to work, but its absence; and to feel its absence it must from time to time pass through me" (*OC* VIII, 26). In the same fragment Artaud provides an insight into the effect of his disability—and of opium—on his sexuality: "Virility is intermittent . . . everything comes in periods. At times there is the sensuality of a Mammoth . . . at others the sufferer is an angel, a priest, a pitiful sacristan" (*OC* VIII, 27). It is surely significant that later, when he was constructing his antisex mythology, Artaud claimed that his body had been invaded by an angel.

The vast conspiracy of "initiates" who, he believed in his years of confinement, had put him under a terrible spell was, among other things, concerned with denying him access to opium. The intoxicating power of opium itself, he explained in his letters from Rodez, was the result of a spell that had been put upon it, while its real object was to make exceptional souls able to transcend themselves. The English had put Chaucer and

Joan of Arc to death and had conducted an opium war in China for that very reason, "because they are whites, and opium is black, and they wanted to exterminate the black" (*OC* IX, 204).

Just as what had initially been mere anger with the authorities who made access to drugs difficult grew and intensified itself in Artaud's mind into a world conspiracy to deny him opium, so his sense of pride in being separated from others by his disability, his suffering, magnified itself first into the image of the Tortured Man of the tarot pack who was to bring deliverance to mankind in *Les Nouvelles Révélations de l'Etre,* and later became the conviction that it was he, Artaud, who had been crucified on Golgotha:

> I was on Golgotha two thousand years ago and my name was, as always, Artaud, and I detested the priests and God, and that was why I was crucified by the priests of Jehovah, as a poet and an enlightened one, and then thrown on a heap of dung. . . . I know that filthy little swine, that terrible little spell-caster of Judaea whom all of today's Christianity adores, and who had himself accepted as resurrected in the light under the name of Jesus-Christ. When in fact he was none other than a certain M. Nalpas. (*OC* IX, 204)

It must be remembered that until shortly before he wrote this text Artaud had insisted on signing all his letters with his mother's maiden name, Nalpas, and had also been excessively pious and assiduous in observing all the rites of the Catholic Church. So *both* his selves claimed to be Jesus Christ.

Violent oscillation of attitudes between extremes is characteristic of Artaud's fantasy life in his last phase. His attitude to sexuality swung from identification with Heliogabalus, that secular incarnation of sexual excess and depravity, to a total, disgusted rejection of sex. The revolutionary who had wanted to use the theater to subvert the existing structure of the bourgeois state assured Paulhan in 1943 that "Religion, Family, and Fatherland are the three things I respect. . . . I have always been a royalist and patriot" (*OC* x, 103-104), and even dedicated a copy of *Les Nouvelles Révélations de l'Etre* to Hitler. He became exceedingly pious and later exceedingly blasphemous. Having been a devoted disciple of the Cabbala and oriental religions, he later became convinced that it was in fact the Jews and the lamas of Tibet who were casting their spells upon him. The image which rationalized these violent changes in his attitudes was that of one self having died while another occupied or usurped the body. He applied the same reasoning to his friends: Those who had disappointed him were no longer the people they had been but were zombies whose bodies were inhabited by evil spirits.

After his release from Rodez Artaud continued to believe in the conspiracy that had put him under a spell. But at the same time, by another characteristic reversal of attitudes, his aggression was now mainly directed against Dr. Ferdière, whom he had assured of his devotion and gratitude on the train journey to Paris, and against psychiatrists and doctors in general.

As his body was increasingly racked by cancer Artaud developed another fascinating dissociation: His aggression turned against his own body. In one of his late poems he accuses the evil, earth-bound God of the Gnostics, the Demiurge, of having usurped his body because he could

> find no better way
> to achieve being
> than to be born at the price
> of my assassination.[1]

He, who had so deeply believed in the mission of the body as the seat of emotion through which life realizes

[1] From a poem in 84, No. 5/6, 1948.

itself to the full, found a way to reconcile that conviction with a violent *hatred* of the body. He developed the belief that while the body, seat of feeling and sensation, was of immense value, it could do without organs, which, far from making up the body, destroy its unity by hurting and constantly obtruding their own obscene individuality. Man's anatomy needs to be completely remade, for

> there is nothing so useless as an organ. Once you have given Man a body without organs, you will have delivered him from all his automatisms and given him back his true freedom. (*OC* xiii, 104)

There is a significant analogy between Artaud's dissociation of the body and its organs and Beckett's limbless heroes who have shed some of their organs in the pursuit of their real selves.

By another and analogous dissociation Artaud, more than ever disgusted by sex and defecation, the organs of which he detested more than any others, used increasingly scatological and obscene language in attacking them. And this disgust with the organs of the body eventually turned into a disgust with existence itself:

> *Where there is a stink of shit*
> *there is a smell of being.* (*OC* xiii, 83)

That rage against his disability which had deprived him of his sense of being in his youth was now transmuted into a fervent wish to be liberated from the pain and distress of being itself.

This brief attempt to list and describe some of the aspects of Artaud's psychological development is not an analysis, nor does it pretend to be anything like a diagnosis of his case. There are those who have categorized his illness as schizophrenia, paraphrenia, paranoia, or religious mania, whether inborn, acquired by physical lesions in early youth, or caused by society's rejection or, indeed, by psychiatric treatment in mental hospitals. Others have seen it as a poet's exaltation and inspired frenzy, which enabled him to provide unique insights into human nature. One or the other of these views, or indeed both, may be true.

What is beyond doubt is that the history of Artaud's psyche, so fully and so eloquently documented, has given considerable impulse to the thinking of our time in the fields of psychology and psychoanalysis and their social applications. Important seminal works like Michel Foucault's *Histoire de la Folie* and Deleuze and Guattari's *L'Anti-Oedipe* make considerable use of insights derived from Artaud, as does the work of R. D. Laing and his associates.

None of the disabilities Artaud suffered or the fantasies and structures of myth he produced are in themselves perhaps very different from those of many other sufferers from similar distressing states of mind. But his genius as a writer, his eloquence, and his descriptive brilliance contribute a great deal to the impact and paradigmatic quality of his case. And here again a further, and mysterious, element enters in: What really gives this highly particular and personal case truly universal significance is, ultimately, Artaud's achievement in wholly *living*, totally incarnating his experience. In that sense he may have been very near the truth when he claimed that he was being crucified to bear the burden of all mankind. His pain, distress, and torment certainly produced an intensity of psychic energy which can still make itself felt in the fervor it continues to inspire and to generate.

Irrationalism, Aggression, Revolution

vi

During the night of 16 May 1968 crowds of insurgent Paris students flooded into the Odéon-Théâtre de France, then under the artistic direction of Jean-Louis Barrault, and occupied the venerable old building. As the first of the revolutionary youths burst into Barrault's office and saw the portrait of Artaud above his desk, he exclaimed: "He has stolen Artaud!"[1]

That young revolutionary, who had never known Artaud, almost certainly had no idea that Barrault had been Artaud's comrade-in-arms, had shared many of his most intimate thoughts, had been his friend and disciple, had responded to his appeals for help in the dark years of his confinement, and was continuing Artaud's work in the theater. To the student revolutionary *that* Artaud did not exist. For him Artaud was the embodiment of his own rejection of society as constituted in 1968, the scourge of the bourgeoisie,

[1] Jean-Louis Brau, *Antonin Artaud,* p. 166n.

the source of a stream of invective and abuse against established institutions. An abstract image of Artaud had swamped the real Artaud, whom Jean-Louis Barrault had known and loved, and was now floating ahead of the teeming masses of rioting young people, a lodestar of their revolt.

Artaud's *Lettre aux Recteurs des Universités Européennes* (*Letter to the Chancellors of Europe's Universities*), which had formed part of Number Three of *La Révolution Surréaliste* (April 1923), had been one of the first leaflets issued by the students of the Sorbonne in May 1968. And although this text, as we now know, was not written entirely by Artaud, being a collaborative effort of the surrealist movement, it made him one of the chief inspirations of the student revolt, whose spirit it fitted to perfection:

> Europe crystallizes and slowly mummifies under the chains of its frontiers, its factories, its law courts, its universities. The frozen Spirit cracks under the slabs of stone which press upon it. It's the fault of your moldy systems, your logic of two and two makes four, it is your fault, University Chancellors, caught in the nets of your own syllogisms. You produce engineers, judges, doctors unable to grasp the true mysteries of the body, the cosmic laws of being, false scientists blind to the world beyond the Earth, philosophers who pretend they can reconstruct the Spirit. . . . Leave us alone, gentlemen, you are nothing but usurpers. By what right do you pretend to canalize intelligence, to award diplomas of the Spirit? (*OC* 1, 335-36)

Shortly after Artaud had produced this letter and others equally aggressive and denunciatory to the Pope, the Dalai Lama, and the Schools of Buddha, he broke with the surrealists precisely because they had decided to translate their revolutionary attitude into action by joining the Communist party, while Artaud obstinately maintained that political action was useless and true revolution could come only by a transformation of the human consciousness and spirit from within. Convinced as he was throughout his life—this is the one strand of total consistency that runs through his *oeuvre* —that it was the spirit of rationalism, analytic and discursive thought, formal logic, and linguistic pedantry which had desiccated the fullness of Man's emotional life and cut him off from the profound sources of his vital being, Artaud rejected revolutionary Marxism as simply another form of rationalism. "The Communist revolution ignores the inner world of thought," he declared in one of his lectures in Mexico (1936); European civilization had to be rejected because of its rationalism:

> To find its profound nature again, to feel itself live in its thought, Life rejects the spirit of analysis in which Europe has gone astray. Poetic knowledge is internal, the poetic quality is internal. There is a movement today which aims at identifying the poetry of the poets with the magical inner force which carves a way for Life and allows us to have an influence on Life. Whether thought is a secretion of matter or not—I don't want to spend time on discussing the question. I shall simply say that the materialism of Lenin seems in fact to ignore this Poetics of thought."
> (*OC* VIII, 191-92)

Hence "the revolution invented by Marx is a caricature of Life" (*OC* VIII, 184). In notes for another lecture or article for Mexico he put the matter even more succinctly: "Have come to Mexico/to flee Barbarity of Europe/last example of European Barbarity: Marxism" (*OC* VIII, 157).

The student revolutionaries of 1968—and the adherents to the new revolutionary counterculture which reached its peak around 1970 and has been on the wane since the mid-1970s—also rejected Marxism in its rationalist and "scientific" guise. Hence Artaud's image as an antirationalist, drug-addicted mystic and visionary believer in the Cabbala, the tarot, and eastern religions was particularly attractive and potent for them. To fashion that image they had to fuse elements from his thought and writings from different periods of his career into a highly unhistorical amalgam: Taking quotations from texts from a period when Artaud *did* believe in the Cabbala and the Tibetan Book of the Dead, they had to ignore his vehement denunciation of mysticism and Oriental cults during a later period, from which, however, even more violent denunciations of established civilization (like the nightmare of school-boys' sperm being deep-frozen for the future production of American cannon fodder) admirably served the anti-American *Zeitgeist*. Yet, undoubtedly, the chief appeal of Artaud for the revolutionary counterculture was the vehemence of his denunciations, whatever the target at which they were directed, the violence of his vituperative rhetoric.

It is as though Artaud's pent-up frustrations, which had exploded in writing of unparalleled aggressiveness, retained their power beyond the grave and were able to engender and energize aggressive forces of a similar nature across space and time. So great were the psychic energies stored in Artaud's brilliantly written poetic outbursts, so powerful was his style, so potent his expressive force that, like the initial release of energy in an atomic bomb, they were able to unleash a veritable chain reaction in the minds of countless individuals who in turn inspired similar aggressive sentiments in scores of others they encountered on their paths.

Ironically enough, all those who knew him intimately agree that in his personal life Artaud was an exceptionally mild, sweet-natured man. All the more powerfully, it seems, did his suppressed aggressions issue into his writings. Only in one sphere, that of the theater, was he ever concerned with propounding a *positive* vision: His proposals may in some respects have been impractical or difficult to implement, but they were constructive and amounted to an alternative blueprint. But when it came to the iniquities of the contemporary established social order and culture, Artaud's criticism was purely negative. He denounced industrial civilization, machines, science, medicine, the pedantries of the law; but all he could advocate to replace them was a vague idea about returning to the Middle Ages, ancient Mexican civilization, or—at certain points in his career—the supposedly happier life-styles of ancient China or Tibet. Such preponderance of negative over positive ideas, however, was also the hallmark of the new counterculture. It is, after all, inherent in any irrational or antirational attitude that a rational thinking-out of the tactics and goals of the movement would be a contradiction in terms and would reintroduce the self-same analytical method which it is its aim to transcend. Let the old order crumble and be swept away and the sweetness and light of a new utopia will instantly, as if by *magic*, be restored! Hence the emphasis on magic in Artaud's anticipation of a great cosmic upheaval at the time of his adventure with St. Patrick's cane. The revolutionary movement of 1968 acted on very similar principles. Its adherents also believed in the release of spontaneous creative forces (which, to a certain degree, actually occurred) and a transformation of society by these creative energies (which did not occur).

The danger of such a surrender to the Dionysiac life force and its creative ecstasy lies in the blindness of such raptures. It is energy without a defined direction or aim, and ultimately might lead to violence as an end in itself.

Artaud, always the complete incarnation of his own thought, exemplifies precisely these dangers in a paradigmatic fashion. During the war Artaud dedicated a copy of his *Les Nouvelles Révélations de l'Etre* to Hitler (another believer in the right of the individual to follow his inspiration, however violent), and his aggressiveness was directed against vast conspiracies of Jews, Jesuits, British Secret Service agents, and other favorite targets of the political lunatic fringe of the Right as well as the Left. The violent anti-Americanism of his last broadcast was a direct continuation of the same tendency to look for an explanation of history in secret societies and wicked conspiracies. On 6 August 1947 Artaud told Jacques Prevel that "seven to eight hundred million human beings . . . should be exterminated; what is that to the three or four thousand million who inhabit the earth. Most human beings spend their life in doing nothing, exploiting the life of others, taking hold of their consciousness."[2]

Blind aggressiveness on this scale, albeit only in the mind of a dying poet indulging luxuriant daydreams, is closely akin to the ideologies that were realized in the genocide perpetrated by the totalitarian rulers of our time, whether on the Right or the Left, fascist, Nazi, or communist. In the ambivalence of his blind aggressiveness Artaud incarnated and anticipated the ultimate absence of distinction between such labels and ideological colors in the face of destruction on that scale. Whether, in his confinement at Rodez, he was claiming that Breton, the surrealist who had led his movement into the bosom of the Communist party, had fought to free him from arrest at the quayside of Le Havre side by side with battalions of the extreme right-wing Action Française against a Jewish-controlled French police force; or whether he was denouncing the whole of Western, bourgeois culture, surely a right-wing phenomenon, as doomed to utter destruction, Artaud was merely letting his frustration, rage, and destructive fervor flow, regardless of ideology, into any channel that seemed to offer itself by the chance of the moment. And that, of necessity, is where a cult of emotion for emotion's sake, provided it is deeply felt, of maximum

[2] Jacques Prevel, *En Compagnie d'Antonin Artaud*, p. 168.

intensity, and wholly untrammelled by thought, must ultimately lead.

In *L'Anti-Oedipe*, their brilliant but highly disturbing study of capitalism and schizophrenia, which fuses Freudianism and Marxism on a structuralist basis, Gilles Deleuze and Félix Guattari derive much of their argument from the case history and personality of Artaud, whom they regard both as a paradigmatic, well-documented case and as a kind of saintly model. To them society is at present polarized between the capitalist-fascist attitude—gregarious, rejoicing in crowds and the notion of participation in a superior race or nation— which corresponds to the clinical picture of *paranoia*, on the one hand; and on the other, the revolutionary attitude—that of the isolated, despised outcast, cut off from the crowd, withdrawing into his inner self—which presents the phenotype of *schizophrenia*. But if the revolutionary, in his hatred of organized society, develops his aggressiveness against it to fever pitch, and if, as Deleuze and Guattari clearly advocate, the revolutionaries unite in concerted action against society, then, surely, schizophrenia has itself become paranoia and the revolutionary attitude is merely the reverse side of the coin which has fascism on its obverse. Deleuze and Guattari explicitly recognize that "the two poles are united in Artaud's magic formula: Heliogabalus—the anarchist."[3] And, indeed, Artaud exemplifies the profound identity of all political attitudes based on the primacy of emotion over reason and their inevitable resort to violently aggressive action.

The use made of Artaud's image in France and elsewhere by a wide variety of different movements and causes clearly illustrates this state of affairs. In France, whose cultural life has long been dominated by a philosophy of sweet reasonableness, a fine balance between emotion and the intellect, a belief in the middle way,

[3] Gilles Deleuze and Félix Guattari, *L'Anti-Oedipe*, p. 330.

self-control, and action based on logic, Artaud's rejection of the Apollonian principle in favor of the unrestrained ecstasies of Dionysus has rallied a whole generation eager to reject the traditions of a past which has gone stale and become boring. The example of Artaud is to them a welcome model; it shows that emotion released from all restraint of logic, from any need to seek empirical endorsement of its conclusions, can result in a glorious rhetoric of unbridled passion. Much of what goes by the name of philosophy or political science in France today is, basically, just such Artaudian rhetoric, words used for their emotional charge, the sensuous impact of their sound rather than their meaning. That Artaud's writings, oscillating as they do between the most contradictory positions, enable him to be quoted at will in support of any emotional or "ideological" stance is another important point in their favor. Orthodox Catholics can use him as readily as Maoists: There is a delicious essay proving that Artaud and Mao Tse-tung are ultimately one, in the volume chronicling the proceedings of a symposium on Artaud held by the *Tel Quel* group in 1972. The argument is simple: Artaud liked the Orient; China is the Orient; Mao Tse-tung is Chinese—ergo Artaud is a Maoist.[4] Similarly Artaud, who at times denounced opium as a pernicious and evil thing and at others clamored for it, has become one of the chief idols of the American drug-culture, whose tactics include turning street violence or the conduct of a trial like that of the Chicago Seven into theatrical Happenings, street and court room theater.

To record the fact that Artaud and his writings have engendered, or have served as a pretext for engendering, violence is not to say that he is to be blamed for that violence or, indeed, for the flood of stupidities which are

[4] Jacques Henric, *Artaud travaillé par la Chine* in *Artaud*, ed. Philippe Sollers.

proclaimed by would-be disciples. Here too Artaud's fate is that of every Master whose message is incarnated in his life rather than in a coherent body of work. The image, or fragments of the image, becomes detached from the personality as an organic whole and assumes a life of its own. As Artaud postulated for the theater, a powerful image releases emotions, body sensations, in those who are exposed to it; but who can tell what those emotions will amount to, in what action they may result? The beauty of Artaud, the monk ministering to St. Joan on the stake, may engender devotion; the ravaged features of Artaud, the martyr of Rodez, may arouse pity and anger at the society who made him suffer; but once those emotions are transformed into energies of belief or action, they may well be far removed from what Artaud himself felt, thought, and stood for. Precisely because Artaud's ideas are totally incarnated in Artaud's life and personality, they make sense only in the context of his own experience, above all his own suffering. His rage and aggressiveness are, ultimately, merely poetic metaphors for his suffering and can only be understood as complementary to it. *He* had the right to utter those heart-rending screams of pain we can still hear in his last recording, because he suffered the pain from which they sprang. But that does not give others, who have not felt that pain, the justification to start uttering equally loud and strident cries. Without the suffering such screams are hollow, empty, superficial, and fake. And what is true of the screams is equally true of violent talk and violent action. The middle-class student revolutionaries of the Paris riots of May 1968 who used Artaud's aggressiveness to power their own frustrations did not share these sufferings but merely exploited them for their own shallow ends and to provide cheap thrills for themselves. In that sense, they, not Jean-Louis Barrault, had stolen Artaud.

Conclusion

VII

Antonin Artaud, the man who lived and suffered and raged and was loved by his friends, is dead. He no longer exists. But the residue of his existence—a million words in a long row of collected works and letters; his drawings; the shape of his body still moving in his films; the strident tones of his voice on the tapes he recorded—all that is still alive and active. And like that corpse in Ionesco's play which keeps on growing, Artaud's remains also are still expanding: Around his own *oeuvre* there accumulate the reminiscences of those who knew him, the commentaries and explanations, the tracts which exhort this or that group or type of his followers and disciples to emulate his actions or to live by his image and example.

Most people, when they die, leave something behind—possessions, memories, writings; but these gradually fade away and lose their impact. Even the work of important thinkers or scientists is gradually absorbed into the general stream of established knowledge and, by becoming commonplace, gradually dissolves the individuality and personal influence of the men themselves. The cases in which the *personality* rather than the *oeuvre* or achievement of an important figure continues to increase in its impact are very rare. Only the founders of religions can genuinely claim such powerful and expanding potency. Artaud was not—or has at least not yet become—the founder of a religion. But he has become the center of a cult or, indeed, several cults. And as such he has something in common with the founders of religions. As he did not aim to create an *oeuvre* so much as to make his own life his supreme work of art and thus to incarnate his ideas rather than merely express them, he engenders, not the appreciation given to great artists, but the devotion due to a beloved individual. And the very contradictoriness, dissociation, even incoherence of his ideas merely strengthen such primarily emotional devotion, which must ultimately lead to a cult. An ideology can be disproved and discredited; a work of poetry, painting, or music can be criticized; but a *person* can merely be loved or rejected. And those who love such a personality love him with all his contradictions. The presence of the personality, however, its continued presence, is ensured by the intensity of the psychic energy enshrined in the manifestations of its activity which have remained with posterity. And Artaud not only had that exceptional potency of psychic energy, he also had the gift of projecting it in a fashion which is more than supreme artistic craftsmanship, which, indeed, in the spontaneity and directness which puts it beyond the bounds of aesthetic analysis as art, is akin to magic. In this sense Artaud's concept of the theater is completely vindicated by the manner in which he succeeded in transforming his own life into a dream, his own personality into a unique theatrical character, a character however whose sufferings were *real*, portrayed by an *actor* who had the supreme skill of transmitting to his audience the strength, intensity, and color of his emotions by a process akin to that vibration of the soil through which the snake-charmer in Artaud's simile imposes his emotion on the coils of the snake's body. The plays Artaud wrote and produced were far from perfect, but his own life was the perfect tragedy, perfectly enacted. That is why its impact continues beyond the grave.

The cults through which Artaud's psychic energy remains intense and active may, in themselves, be silly, shallow, or intellectually feeble. This is not to say that one of them may not gradually, as a tradition coagulates around it, turn into a powerful current, become the basis of some sort of religion. History knows examples of this kind of phenomenon.

On a more mundane and secular level, however, Artaud, unlike some other personalities around whom cults have grown up, is unique in the fullness of the documentation he has provided about his life and in the fascinating general implications of his case. In the completeness of his self-revelation he joins the select group of great masters whose genre cannot be classed as mere art but is the full presentation of human life experience itself: Pepys, Casanova, the Marquis de Sade, the Marquise de Sevigné, Boswell, Horace Walpole . . .

Artaud lacks the serenity and inner calm of most of these—the Marquis de Sade is the obvious exception—but, on the other hand, he presents a more extravagantly fascinating psychological, or even psychopathological, case history. He himself saw himself as one of a long line of *poètes maudits*: Hölderlin, Baudelaire, Nerval, Lautréamont, Nietzsche. And he was undoubtedly right. Yet none of these has left as full and enlightening a documentation of himself as that which Artaud has left to posterity.

But Artaud transcends the category of the *poètes maudits* as well as that of the great self-revealers. For he provides an immense wealth of detailed insights into a human type of the utmost importance in history.

Artaud's life was a fascinating anachronism in our times but all the more valuable through the material it furnishes us with about this crucially influential kind of character: the character, that is, of the "Holy Fool." It was Artaud's misfortune that he was born into an epoch which consigns individuals of this stamp to lunatic asylums. In other epochs he might have been a shaman, a prophet, an alchemist, an oracle, a saint, a gnostic teacher, or, indeed, the founder of a new religion. The intensity of his emotion, the depth of his commitment, the rich flow of his myth-making faculty, the eloquence of his language, his all-powerful urge to create ritual (for that, essentially, was the nature of his fanaticism for the theater), the terrifying violence of his invective, the grandiose craziness of his exaltation, all these were present in personalities who, in other epochs, were revered, adored, and martyred as divinely inspired or diabolically possessed vessels of powers transcending the bounds of mere humanity.

Artaud's fate in our time may be a mark of our enlightenment or a disturbing symptom of our spiritual poverty. But whether it is the one or the other, the fate, the martyrdom, the clinical case of Antonin Artaud, Artaud-le-Momo, the holy fool, is a touchstone of our civilization.

ARTAUD'S LIFE: A
BIOGRAPHICAL NOTE

1896	4 September: Artaud born in Marseilles.
1901	Suffers an attack of "meningitis."
1905	21 August: Death of Artaud's infant sister Germaine (born 13 January).
1906	Almost drowns while staying at Smyrna with his maternal grandmother.
1910	At the Collège du Sacré Coeur, starts a literary review and publishes first poems under the pseudonym Louis des Attides.
1915	Destroys all his writings and gives away his books. Spends his first period in a sanatorium.
1916	Called up for military service at Digne. Released after nine months on medical grounds.
1916–18	Periods at sanatoria and health resorts. Stay at Bagneres-de-Bigorre (Pyrenées).
End 1918–20	At the sanatorium of Le Chanet near Neufchatel, Switzerland, under the care of Dr. Dardel.
1919	May: Begins to take laudanum.
1920	March: Arrives in Paris. August: *Demain* publishes a poem and an article by Artaud. Late autumn: Lugné Poe offers him a part at the Théâtre de l'Oeuvre.
1921	17 February: First appearance as an actor in

Henri de Régnier's *Les Scrupules de Sganarelle* at the Théâtre de l'Oeuvre. October: Through his uncle Louis Nalpas, obtains an audition with Firmin Gémier, who recommends him to Charles Dullin. Dullin offers him work with his workshop, the Atelier. Late autumn: In Dullin's company meets and falls in love with Genica Athanasiou (1897–1966).

1922   2 March: Plays King Galvan in Arnoux's *Moriano et Galvan,* for which he also designs scenery and costumes. 20 June: Plays Basilio in Calderón's *Life Is a Dream,* for which he also designs scenery and costumes. July: Sees a troupe of Cambodian dancers at the Marseilles Colonial Exhibition. October: Dullin's company becomes the Théâtre de l'Atelier. 20 December: Plays Tiresias in Cocteau's *Antigone.*

1923   Edits an anthology of Dr. Toulouse's writings, *Au fil des préjugés.* 2 February: Publication of first number of Artaud's literary periodical, *Le Bilboquet.* 15 February: Appears in the part of a grotesque puppet in J. Grau's *Monsieur Pygmalion* at the Théâtre de l'Atelier. April: Joins Pitoeff's troupe at the Comédie des Champs-Elysées. 1 May: Start of the correspondence with Jacques Rivière (concluded 8 June 1924). 4 May: First volume of poems, *Tric-Trac du ciel,* published by Kahnweiler. 26 December: Plays Jackson in Andreyev's *He Who Gets Slapped* at the Comédie des Champs-Elysées.

1924   26 March: Plays a robot in Capek's *RUR* at the Comédie des Champs-Elysées. April: Acts in Claude Autant-Lara's film *Faits divers.* Summer: works in Brittany in Luitz-Morat's film *Surcouf.* Visits Berlin to work with UFA. 1 September: Publication of the correspondence with Rivière in *Nouvelle Revue Française.* 7 September: Death of Artaud's father. His mother moves to Paris. October: Joins the surrealist movement.

1925   15 January: Contributes to No. 2 of *La Révolution Surréaliste.* 26 January: Becomes director of the surrealists' Bureau de Recherches. 15 April:

Appearance of No. 3 of *La Révolution Surréaliste*, edited and almost entirely written by Artaud. 28 and 29 May: Directs Aragon's *Au pied du mur* at the Vieux Colombier. 3-11 June: Works in Marcel Vandal's film *Graziella* on location in Italy. Visits Pompeii and Rome. 23 July: *L'Ombilic des Limbes* published. 1 August: *Le Pèse-Nerfs* published. Trips to Carteret (Manche) with Roger Vitrac. August: Acts in Luitz-Morat's film *Le Juif errant*.

1926   Foundation of the Théâtre Alfred Jarry. November: First Manifesto of the Théâtre Alfred Jarry in the *Nouvelle Revue Française*. End of November: Break with the surrealists.

1927   Spring: Contacts with Jacques Maritain. Acts in Abel Gance's film *Napoléon*, in which he plays Marat. 1 and 2 June: First performances of the Théâtre Alfred Jarry at the Théâtre de la Grenelle. June: Carl Theodor Dreyer offers him the part of the young monk in *La Passion de Jeanne d'Arc*. Tries psychoanalytic treatment with Dr. René Allendy. October: Acts in Léon Poirier's film *Verdun, visions d'histoire*. November: The *NRF* publishes his scenario for the film *La Coquille et le clergyman*. December: Visits Cannes.

1928   14 January: Second production of the Théâtre Alfred Jarry at the Comédie des Champs-Elysées. 18 February: First performance of *La Coquille et le clergyman* at the Studio des Ursulines. 22 March: Lectures at the Sorbonne on *L'Art et la mort*. 2 and 9 June: Third production of the Théâtre Alfred Jarry: Strindberg's *Dream Play*. Acts in Marcel Herbier's film *L'Argent* (after Zola). 24 and 29 December: Fourth and last production of the Théâtre Alfred Jarry: Roger Vitrac's *Victor*.

1929   February–April: Acts in film *Tarakanova*, directed by Raymond Bernard at the Nice studios. 26 April: Registers his adaptation of R. L. Stevenson's *The Master of Ballantrae*. 17 April: *L'Art et la mort* published by Denoël.

1930   July–August and October: In Berlin to work on

films, notably Pabst's version of Brecht's *Three-penny Opera*.

1931   January–May: Acts in Raymond Bernard's films *Faubourg Montmartre* and *Les Crois de Bois,* and in Marcel Herbier's *La Femme de Nuit.* July: Sees Balinese Dancers at the Colonial Exhibition in the Bois de Vincennes. End of liaison with Josette Lusson. Publication of his free translation of M. Lewis's *The Monk.* 10 December: Lectures at the Sorbonne on *La Mise-en-scène et la métaphysique.*

1932   February: *La Mise-en-scène et la métaphysique* published in the *NRF.* Project for a theater sponsored by the *NRF.* February–March: Assists Louis Jouvet in production of Alfred Savoir's *La Patissière du village.* April–May: In Berlin to act in Serge de Poligny's film *Coup de feu à l'aube.* Adapts Seneca's *Atreus and Thyestes.* October: "First Manifesto of the Theater of Cruelty" published in the *NRF.* December: In hospital for a disintoxication treatment.

1933   March: Beginning of friendship with Anais Nin. April: Completes *Héliogabale.* 6 April: Lectures at the Sorbonne on *Le Théâtre et la peste.* "Second Manifesto of the Theater of Cruelty."

1934   Reads scenario for *La Conquête du Mexique* at a soirée to raise funds for the Theater of Cruelty. Publication of *Héliogabale.* Summer: On location in Algeria to film *Sidonie Panache,* directed by Henri Wullschleger. Also acts in *Liliom,* directed by Fritz Lang; *Koenigsmarck,* directed by Marcel Tourneur; *Lucrèce Borgia,* directed by Abel Gance, in which he gives a memorable performance as Savonarola. October: *NRF* publishes *Le Théâtre et la peste.*

1935   6 May: *Les Cenci* opens at the Folies-Wagram. Autumn: Meets Cécile Schramme.

1936   January: Leaves Paris for Antwerp, and sails to Havána. 7 February: Disembarks at Santa Cruz. April: Leaves Mexico City for the Sierra Tarahumara, whence he returns in October. 31 October: Leaves Mexico. Writes *Les Nouvelles Révélations de l'Etre.* Engagement to Cécile Schramme.

1937   March: Disintoxication treatment in Paris. April: Renewed disintoxication cure at Sceaux. 20 May: Disastrous lecture at Brussels; engagement to Cécile Schramme broken off. 28 July: *Les Nouvelles Révélations de l'Etre* published as an anonymous pamphlet. 1 August: *D'un voyage au pays des Tarahumaras* published anonymously in the *NRF*. 14 August: Arrives in Ireland at Cobh. 17 August: Leaves Galway for the Aran Islands. 2 September: At Imperial Hotel, Galway. 8 September: Leaves Galway for Dublin. 30 September: Arrives at Le Havre on S.S. *Washington*, under detention and in a straitjacket. Handed to French authorities.

1938   7 February: *Le Théâtre et son double* published. 12 April: Transferred to asylum of Sainte-Anne, Paris. December: At the asylum of Quatre-Mares, Sotteville-lès-Rouen.

1939   27 February: Transferred to asylum at Ville Evrard.

1943   22 January: Temporary transfer to the "rural" asylum at Chézal-Benoît. 11 February: Arrives at asylum of Rodez (Aveyron) and is put in the care of Dr. Gaston Ferdière.

1944   10 May: Reissue of *Le Théâtre et son double*.

1945   25 November: *Au pays des Tarahumaras* appears as a book.

1946   19 March: Released from Rodez asylum for a short stay in the neighborhood. 8 April: *Lettres de Rodez* published by *GLM*. 26 May: Takes up residence as a voluntary patient at Dr. Delmas's mental hospital at Ivry. 6 June: Opening of exhibition of works by leading painters, donated to raise funds for Artaud. 7 June: Benefit performance on Artaud's behalf at the Théâtre Sarah-Bernhardt.

1947   13 January: Artaud appears at the Vieux Colombier in a series of poetry readings, *"Tête-à-tête."* January: Visits van Gogh exhibition at the Orangerie. 19 July: Reads his poetry at Galerie Pierre, where an exhibition of his drawings is held. 15 September: Official publication date of

Le Retour d'Artaud-le-Momo; 25 September: Official publication date of *Van Gogh le suicidé de la société* (the two books available ca. 15 December). 22–29 November: Recording of *Pour en finir avec le jugement de Dieu*.

1948   5 February: *Pour en finir avec le jugement de Dieu* recommended for broadcast. 4 March: Found dead. 8 March: Buried without rites at the cemetery of Ivry.

SHORT BIBLIOGRAPHY

ARTAUD'S WRITINGS

The collected edition of Artaud's works and letters is the *Oeuvres Complètes* (Paris: Gallimard, 1956–). Of this, fourteen volumes had appeared by the end of 1975, i.e. volumes I-XIII and a supplementary volume to volume I. Volumes I-III, originally published in 1956 and 1961, have been reissued in a revised and augmented form as volume I, 1970; Supplement to volume I, 1970; volume II, 1973.

There is, in addition, a volume of letters, *Lettres à Genica Athanasiou* (Paris: Gallimard, 1969).

The fullest bibliography of Artaud's writings scattered in pamphlets and periodicals can be found in Alain Virmaux's book listed below.

TRANSLATIONS

An English edition of Artaud's collected works is appearing in London, translated by Victor Corti (London: Calder & Boyars, 1968–). Of this four volumes had appeared by the end of 1975.

In the United States *The Theater and Its Double* is available in a translation by C. Richards (New York: Grove Press, 1958).

An excellent selection of Artaud's poems and late essays is the *Antonin Artaud Anthology*, edited by Jack Hirschman (San Francisco: City Light Books, 1965).

SPECIAL NUMBERS OF PERIODICALS DEVOTED TO ARTAUD

Cahiers de la Compagnie Renaud-Barrault, No. 22-23, May 1958.
La Tour de Feu, Jarnac (Charente) No. 63-64, December 1959.
La Tour de Feu, No. 69, April 1961.
La Tour de Feu, No. 112, December 1971.
Tulane Drama Review, No. 22, Winter 1963.
Tel Quel, No. 20, Winter 1965.
Tel Quel, No. 52, Winter 1972.

BOOKS ABOUT ARTAUD

Armand-Laroche, Dr. J.-L. *Antonin Artaud et son double*. Périgueux: Pierre Fanlac, 1964.

Barrault, Jean-Louis. *Souvenirs pour demain*. Paris: Editions du Seuil, 1972.

Blanchot, Maurice. *Le livre à venir*. Paris: Gallimard, 1959.

Brau, Jean-Louis. *Antonin Artaud*. Paris: La Table Ronde, 1971.

Bugard, Pierre. *Le Comédien et son double*. Paris: Stock, 1970.

Charbonnier, Georges. *Essai sur Antoine Artaud*. Paris: Seghers, 1959.

Deleuze, Gilles and Guattari, Félix. *L'Anti-Oedipe*. Paris: Editions de Minuit, 1972.

Derrida, Jacques. *L'Ecriture et la différence*. Paris: Editions du Seuil, 1967.

Durozoi, Gérard. *Artaud: l'aliénation et la folie*. Paris: Larousse, 1972.

Foucault, Michel. *Histoire de la folie*. Paris: Plon, 1961.

Greene, Naomi. *Antonin Artaud: Poet without Words*. New York: Simon and Schuster, 1970.

Gouhier, Henri. *Antonin Artaud et l'essence du théâtre.* Paris: Vrin, 1974.

Hahn, Otto. *Portrait d'Antonin Artaud.* Paris: Soleil Noir, 1968.

Hort, Jean, *Antonin Artaud, le suicide de la société.* Geneva: Editions Connaître, 1960.

Knapp, Bettina L. *Antonin Artaud, Man of Vision.* New York: Discus Books, 1971.

Matthews, J. H. *Theater in Dada and Surrealism.* Syracuse: University Press, 1974.

Nin, Anais. *The Journals of Anais Nin.* 5 vols. London: Peter Owen, 1966-1974.

Prevel, Jacques. *En Compagnie d'Antonin Artaud.* Paris: Flammarion, 1974.

Sollers, Philippe (ed.). *Artaud.* Paris: 10/18, 1973.

Sellin, Eric. *The Dramatic Concepts of Antonin Artaud.* Chicago: University of Chicago Press, 1968.

Tonnelli, Franco. *L'Esthétique de la cruauté.* Paris: Nizet, 1972.

Virmaux, Alain. *Antonin Artaud et le théâtre.* Paris: Seghers, 1970.

INDEX